Asatru

The Ultimate Guide to Norse Paganism, Heathenry, and Asatru for Beginners

© Copyright 2021

The contents of this book may not be reproduced, duplicated or transmitted without direct written permission from the author.

Under no circumstances will any legal responsibility or blame be held against the publisher for any reparation, damages, or monetary loss due to the information herein, either directly or indirectly.

Legal Notice:

This book is copyright protected. This is only for personal use. You cannot amend, distribute, sell, use, quote or paraphrase any part or the content within this book without the consent of the author.

Disclaimer Notice:

Please note the information contained within this document is for educational and entertainment purposes only. Every attempt has been made to provide accurate, up to date and reliable complete information. No warranties of any kind are expressed or implied. Readers acknowledge that the author is not engaging in the rendering of legal, financial, medical or professional advice. The content of this book has been derived from various sources. Please consult a licensed professional before attempting any techniques outlined in this book.

By reading this document, the reader agrees that under no circumstances is the author responsible for any losses, direct or indirect, which are incurred as a result of the use of information contained within this document, including, but not limited to, —errors, omissions, or inaccuracies.

Your Free Gift (only available for a limited time)

Thanks for getting this book! If you want to learn more about various spirituality topics, then join Mari Silva's community and get a free guided meditation MP3 for awakening your third eye. This guided meditation mp3 is designed to open and strengthen ones third eye so you can experience a higher state of consciousness. Simply visit the link below the image to get started.

https://spiritualityspot.com/meditation

Contents

INTRODUCTION 1
CHAPTER 1: WHAT IS NORSE PAGANISM? 3
    Understanding Norse Paganism, Its Roots, and Expansion 3
    Textual Sources for Norse Paganism 6
    Toponymic and Archeological Evidence 8
    Expansion of Norse Paganism 8
    Beliefs of Norse Paganism 9
    Cosmology in Norse Paganism 10
    Afterlife in Norse Paganism 11
    The Decline of Norse Paganism 12
    The Concept of Paganism 13
CHAPTER 2: THE OLD WAYS – THE VIKINGS AND THE ANGLO-SAXONS 14
    Viking Paganism 14
    Belief Systems of the Vikings 17
    Anglo-Saxon Paganism 19
CHAPTER 3: HEATHENRY VS. ASATRU 23
    The Origins and History of Heathenry 24
    Understanding Asatru 26
    Understanding Heathenism and Asatru 26
    The Asatru Association 27

THE BLOT RITUAL 28
  ASATRU PERSPECTIVES 29
CHAPTER 4: THE NINE NOBLE VIRTUES AND OTHER CODES 32
  THE NINE NOBLE VIRTUES 33
  THE NINE CHARGES 41
CHAPTER 5: THE AESIR, VANIR, AND JOTNAR 42
  CREATION MYTH OF NORSE MYTHOLOGY 42
  THE AESIR AND VANIR 43
  NORSE DEITIES 44
CHAPTER 6: ASATRU AND NATURE 55
  UNRAVELING THE VAETTIR 55
  WIGHTS IN SCANDINAVIAN FOLKLORE 56
  OTHER NATURE SPIRITS 61
CHAPTER 7: YGGDRASIL AND THE NINE WORLDS 63
  THE YGGDRASIL 65
  MUSPELHEIM 66
  NIFLHEIM 66
  ASGARD 67
  VANAHEIM 68
  JOTUNHEIM 68
  ALFHEIM 69
  MIDGARD 69
  HELHEIM 70
  SVARTALFHEIM 71
CHAPTER 8: HEATHEN RITUALS, SHAMANS, AND SONGS 72
  THE BLOT 72
  A SIMPLE GUIDE TO A BLOT RITUAL 76
  SUMBEL 83
  SEIDR AND GALDR 85
  FESTIVALS OF HEATHENISM 86
CHAPTER 9: CELEBRATE LIKE A HEATHEN – HOLIDAYS AND FESTIVALS 87
  YULE OR YULETIDE – THE 12-DAY FESTIVAL 88
  DISTING 89

    Ostara – March 20th–21st 89
    Walpurgis Night or May Eve 90
    Midsummer – Summer Solstice June 20th–21st 91
    Freyfest or Lammas or Lithasblot – July 31st–August 1st 92
    Fallfest or Mabon – Autumn Equinox 92
    Harvestfest or Winter Nights – October 31st 93
    Other Festivals and Remembrance Days in Heathenism 94

CHAPTER 10: PRACTICING ASATRU TODAY 96
    Finding Fellow-Asatruars 100
    The Kindred List 101
    Worldwide Map of Asatru 104

CONCLUSION 105

HERE'S ANOTHER BOOK BY MARI SILVA THAT YOU MIGHT LIKE 107

YOUR FREE GIFT (ONLY AVAILABLE FOR A LIMITED TIME) 108

REFERENCES 109

Introduction

Our beautiful universe is sacred and vastly diverse, and in this diversity it contains opportunities for limitless joy. Different tribes across the globe have their own belief systems and religions, which helped them make sense of their world. Further, the belief systems provide a moral and ethical framework for the followers to live a meaningful and fulfilling life in harmony with their community and nature.

Asatru is a religion involving the belief systems taken from old, pre-Christian Germanic traditions. Also referred to as "Odinism," it is believed to be the natural religion of the Indo-European (also called Germanic) people, before the advent of Christianity.

Asatru involves worshipping and paying tributes and offerings to the ancient Germanic gods, goddesses, deities, and other supernatural beings. A person who practices Asatru is called an Asatruar, and sometimes called a heathen too. Other names of Asatru are Germanic or Norse Paganism, Wodanism, etc.

Now, the above paragraph is only a tiny scratch on the vast and fascinating subject of Asatru. This religion and belief system goes far deeper and is believed to have its origins many thousands of years ago. While the subject is vast, the sources available on the subject can be mind-boggling. Various books speak in isolation about certain topics under Asatru, and many sources are comprehensive.

This book is written for someone who wants to get a better understanding of this marvelous subject—ranging from its origins right up to modern times. You will find everything you need to know about Asatru within the pages of this book. Nearly all your questions about Asatru will be answered here.

One of the best things about Asatru is that it is a great private religion. You can be an Astruar, and no one else needs to know about your beliefs but you. You are free to choose what attracts you to Asatru. And yet, numerous kindred groups all over the world offer you a sense of identity and connection with other practicing Asatruars. In the last chapter, you'll discover how to contact practitioners in your area and even learn how to start your own hearth.

This book contains that kind of information too, such as how to practice Asatru on your own, as well as how to find other practitioners and be part of a like-minded kindred group. The hands-on instructions on how to practice this belief system at home will give you sufficient material to start off immediately, even as you prepare yourself to become part of something larger.

So, read on and know that your fascination for Asatru is only going to deepen by the time you complete this book and understand its various chapters and elements described.

Chapter 1: What is Norse Paganism?

Norse Paganism is also referred to as Old Norse religion. It is the most common term used to refer to a branch of Germanic religion that grew and developed during the Proto-Norse period. Germanic religion or Germanic paganism is a collective term referring to the set of intricately connected religious traditions and cultures of the Germanic people from as far back as the Iron Age, right up to the spread of Christianity. Germanic paganism was an essential element of early German culture.

Understanding Norse Paganism, Its Roots, and Expansion

The Proto-Norse period, sometimes called the Viking Age, refers to around the first century B.C.E., when the Proto-Norse, an Indo-European dialect spoken in the areas in and around the Scandinavian regions, was believed to have evolved. During this period, the North Germanic culture formed as a distinct branch of Germanic culture. Christianity replaced the Old Norse religion between the 8th and the 12th centuries.

Old Norse religion is also referred to by other names, especially among researchers and academicians. These other names include pre-Christian Norse religion, Scandinavian Paganism, Nordic Paganism, Northern Paganism, North Germanic religion, etc. Written texts were non-existent or very rare.

Modern scholars have been able to reconstruct some aspects of Norse Paganism with the help of archaeology, historical linguistics, toponymy, and certain records left behind by the ancient North Germanic peoples like the runic inscriptions. Norse Paganism is classified as an ethnic religion and a "non-indoctrinated community-based belief system," considering that its customs, norms, and practices varied across time, societies, and geographies.

Followers of the Old Norse religion were polytheistic and worshipped and believed in a plethora of gods and goddesses who were divided into two primary groups, namely the Aesir, or "Æsir" in Old Norse, and the Vanir, both of which were equally powerful but were continuously engaged in battles and wars with each other.

The most famous deities of Norse Paganism were Odin and Thor. Other mythical creatures such as giants, land-spirits, and elves also inhabited the world of the gods, according to Norse Paganism. The central theme of Norse Paganism is Yggdrasil, or the world tree. In addition to Midgard—the home of mortals—there are multiple domains, including numerous afterlife realms, which populated the cosmology of Norse Paganism. Each of the realms has a controlling deity.

The tenets, principles, and codes of Norse Paganism were transmitted through oral culture and not in the form of codified or written texts. The Old Norse religion was rife with rituals, ceremonies, and rites. The priests and kings played an important role in performing public sacrificial ceremonies and rituals.

In ancient times, these rituals were performed outdoors in places such as lakes and groves. By the 3rd century C.E., buildings and houses were specifically constructed for these ceremonies. A form of sorcery called Seiðr, which is closely linked to Shamanism, was practiced in the Old Norse religion. The funeral ceremonies of Norse Paganism were quite elaborate. Both cremations and burials were used in the culture and invariably included numerous grave goods.

Right through Norse Paganism's history, vast amounts of trans-cultural diffusions took place, especially with the neighboring cultures. A couple of examples include the Finns, the ancient followers of Finnish Paganism, and Sami, an ancient polytheistic and animistic tradition that, according to anthropologists, is also closely related to Shamanism. The diffusion and variations are largely attributed to the lack of codified texts and dependence on oral transmission of belief systems.

During the Viking Age, the Norse followers from different regions and cultures were more or less a unified entity, thanks especially to the shared Germanic language called Proto-Norse or Old Norse. During this time, Norse Paganism shared ideas and concepts across other cultures, traditions, and languages, which were conditioned by similar ecological, geographical, and cultural factors.

Ethnocultural groups influenced Norse Paganism of the Viking Age through similar traditions, languages, and geographies like:

Balto-Finns – Inhabiting the Baltic Sea region in northern Europe, the Balto-Finns are also referred to as Baltic Sea Finns or Western Finnic peoples. They speak Finnic languages.

Sami – The Sami peoples inhabit the Sapmi region, which forms present-day Sweden, Norway, the Kola Peninsula, and Finland. The Sami people have been commonly referred to as Lapps or Laplanders, a term that is seen as offensive by some Sami people. Therefore, only Sami is used among modern-day scholars.

The ancestors of the Sami people were from the Volga region, Russia, and other Uralic geographies. The Sami people's language is collectively known as Sami languages, a branch of the Uralic language family.

Anglo-Saxons – The Anglo-Saxons lived in England right from the 5th century. This cultural group consisted of Germanic tribes who migrated from continental Europe to England. Their descendants, and other indigenous tribes of England, adopted and imbibed a lot of Anglo-Saxon culture and language. The Anglo-Saxons established the Kingdom of England and helped in growing and developing the English language, which owes a large percentage of words to the language of the Anglo-Saxons.

Greenlandic Inuit – The Greenlandic Inuits are the indigenous people belonging to Greenland and speak the Greenlandic languages, including Kalaallisut, Tunumiit Orassiat or East Greenlandic, and Inuktun or Polar Inuit.

Norse Paganism was completely routed out of existence by Christianity in the 12th century, but some elements were retained as part of the Nordic folklore. Before the advent of Christianity, the practitioners of Norse Paganism did not see the belief system they were following as a religion but more as a way of life, which was incorporated into their daily lives in the form of behavioral attitudes, actions, and rituals. Christianity's arrival generated a conscious need to distinguish the ancient Norse Paganism as a religion separate from Christianity.

Textual Sources for Norse Paganism

Considering Norse Paganism depended far more on oral transmission of its culture and traditions rather than codified texts, very few textual sources are available. Some runic inscriptions survived from Scandinavia. These inscriptions are clearly religious in nature as they contain prayers to Thor, one of the most important Norse gods, to protect objects such as memorial stones. Thor's hammer can also be seen carved in these inscriptions.

While runic inscriptions that have survived the vagaries of time are very few, a considerably large body of historical and religious sources is available. All these texts are Old Norse manuscripts but written in Latin, reflecting the fact that these were codified after Scandinavia was converted to Christianity.

For example, Hávamál is a collection of Old Norse poems transmitted orally right from the Viking Era. According to Norse Paganism, this work contains poems, morals, and ethics, including ritual obligations. Sagas are another form of Norse literature, which contain information about pagan practices and beliefs.

A classic example of a historical saga related to Norse Paganism is Snorri Sturluson's *Heimskringla* and the *Landnámabók*, both of which talk about the early history of Iceland. Snorri Sturluson was an Icelandic poet, politician, and historian of the 12th century who has authored many books and retellings of oral Norse mythology and pagan practices and beliefs. *The Sagas of Icelanders* are prose narratives that have information about Icelandic groups, tribes, and important individuals in Iceland's history. Skaldic poetry is another important literary source that gives us information about the Old Norse religion.

Christians recorded these works of Norse literature, and they were passed on orally until the 12th century, which is when doubt arose about whether they were still accurate representations of ancient Norse Paganism. Most of the Christian chroniclers are believed to have taken a hostile view of the Old Norse religion. Therefore, modern scholars regard these literary sources more as historical fiction rather than verifiable historical records.

Literary sources from regions other than Scandinavia also exist. For example, *Germania,* dating back to around 100 C.E., was written by one of the greatest Roman historians named Tacitus. This book describes the religious beliefs and practices of numerous Germanic tribes.

Toponymic and Archeological Evidence

Considering that most textual sources are seen as historical fiction, archeological and toponymic evidence play an important role in understanding Norse Paganism. Archeological excavations of cult sites and burials especially give us important information about Old Norse religion and culture before conversion to Christianity.

Toponymic evidence relates to place names. For example, names of places with -hof, -horgr, -ve, etc., are typically sites of religious activity. Magnus Olsen, a Norwegian professor of Norse philology at the University of Oslo and linguist of the 20th century, developed a typology of placenames in Norway. He used this system to discover pagan worship places in Norway that included fields, groves, and temple buildings.

Expansion of Norse Paganism

During the Viking Period, Norse people left Scandinavia and settled through northwestern Europe. In the 9th century, they colonized Iceland (a sparsely populated region) and spread their belief system. According to toponymic evidence, Thor was the most popular deity in Iceland, whereas Odin doesn't find a place of prominence. Saga sources suggest the Icelandic settlers worshipped Freyr too.

The Norse people brought their Old Norse religion to Britain around the end of the 9th century. Again, toponymic evidence comes into play here. For example, Roseberry Topping is a site in North Yorkshire. This place was called Othensberg (or Óðinsberg in Old Norse language), "Hill of Odin," in the 12th century. Other place names had references to Norse mythological elements such as alfr, skratii, and troll.

Around the 19th century, there was a revival of interest in Norse Paganism when its various elements, characteristic features, and more, inspired artworks in the Romanticism movement. Around the same time, a lot of academic research work began on the topic, too, thanks to the interest from the art world.

Beliefs of Norse Paganism

Norse mythology consists of stories about Norse gods, goddesses, and deities, which are presented in Eddic poetry. Norse Paganism was a polytheistic culture, and believers prayed to various deities who lived lives similar to human beings, including expressing emotions, marrying, having children, and even dying. For example, Baldr, one of the Norse gods and a son of Odin, dies too.

Not all Norse deities were worshipped. For instance, Loki was an important god in Norse mythology, but there is no evidence of people worshipping him. Though, with new archeological discoveries, new knowledge may come to the fore. It is most likely that the community and the region where people lived directly affected how the different gods and deities were worshipped. Also, each individual treated the gods and goddesses differently. For example, in one skaldic poem of the 10th century, Egill Skallagrimsson describes Odin as a vinr or fulltrui (friend or confidant).

Mythological sources describe two types of deities, namely the Aesir or Æsir, and the Vanir. These two classes of deities fought a bitter war with each other, which ended through a truce and the freeing one another's hostages. The important Æsir deities are Thor, Tyr, and Odin. Some Vanir deities of importance are Njǫrðr, his daughter Freyja, and his son Freyr. Loki's status among this pantheon of gods is not very clear, although Snorri explains that he is buried under the Earth until Ragnarok, a calamitous world event where great wars will be fought, natural disasters will take place, and the world will be submerged in water.

Norse mythology describes deities who originated from giants. Some of these deities are Skaði, Rindr, and Gerðr. Interestingly, the word for goddesses in the Old Norse language is Ásynjur, which is just the feminine version of the word, Æsir. This interpretation could be the reason behind the myth, even though the two classes of deities were equally powerful. Some scholars believe that another Old Norse word for goddess could be dis. This word is used to refer to a collection of female supernatural beings.

Other beings described in Norse mythology include:

- The Norns – female deities who decided people's fates.
- The vættir – land spirits who occupy trees, mountains, waterfalls, rocks, rivers, etc.

Also, there are mentions of levels, dwarfs, guardian spirits, and other deities, many of whom have uncertain stature in the hierarchy. In addition to the above deities, Norse Pagan followers also worshiped local and ancestral spirits and deities. The Finns and Sami people venerate their ancestors through ancestral spirit worship. In some Norwegian tribes, every family had a dedicated family deity.

Cosmology in Norse Paganism

Cosmogonies or creation myths abound in the surviving texts of the mythologies of Norse Paganism. These stories are rife with Nordic gods, goddesses, and other elements.

According to Nordic mythology, before the creation of the universe, there was only a void called Ginnungagap. A giant named Ymir appeared first, after which multiple gods emerged from the void. These gods lifted the earth from out of the sea. Another version of the Nordic creation story talks about the world being created from Ymir's body. His flesh became the earth, his bones became the mountains, his skull was made into the sky, and his blood became the sea.

According to Snorri Sturluson's *Gylfaginning*, the void Ginnungagap existed. Two realms emerged from this void, including the fiery Muspell and the icy Niflheim. Surtr, the fire giant, controlled Muspell. These realms produced a river that coagulated to form Ymir's body. A cow named Audumbla provided Ymir with milk. The cow also licked a big block of ice to free Buri. Buri's son Bor married Bestla, a giantess.

The Yggdrasil, or the cosmic tree, is described as a giant ash tree with three roots, which are home to the goddess Hel, frost-giants, and human beings. Yggdrasil translates to "Odin's Steed." The story of Ragnarok reflects the idea of an inescapable destiny that Nordic people believe in.

Afterlife in Norse Paganism

The Old Norse religion has fully developed concepts of the afterlife. According to Sturluson, there are four realms that the dead people are welcomed into. Interestingly, Norse Paganism did not believe that the morals followed in human life would impact the individual's destination to his or her afterlife.

Warriors who died in battle were taken to Valhalla, Odin's hall, where they waited until Ragnarok when they would battle with the Æsir. Those who died from old age or disease would go to Hel. The other two afterlife realms mentioned by Sturluson were the hall of Brimir and the hall of Sindri. Some Eddic poems talk of the dead living in their graves, remaining conscious there.

The Norse god Odin is most closely associated with death, especially death by hanging. There is a reference to Odin in *The Poetic Edda* to this effect. Odin hanged himself on Yggdrasil for nine nights to gain magical power and wisdom.

The Decline of Norse Paganism

The Nordic people learned about Christianity when they settled in various parts of Europe, including the British Isles, Byzantium (present-day Constantinople), and Novgorod (one of the oldest historic cities in Russia). Therefore, when Christianity came to Scandinavia, it was already an accepted religion. Thus, both Scandinavian migrants and those who remained at home were converted to Christianity very early on, often encouraged by the ruling kings who embraced, patronized, and allowed preachers to convert and spread the new religion.

By the 12th century, Norse Paganism was almost entirely forgotten by the Norse people, although mythological stories survived through oral transmission until the 13th century when they were recorded in written form. Although it is not clear how these old belief systems were passed down orally, scholars believe that there was the possibility of little pockets of pagan believers that retained their belief systems right through the 11th and 12th centuries.

Although the Norse people converted to Christianity, most of them continued to use their mythological motifs and elements in many social and cultural contexts, which ensured that Norse Paganism remained a part of the regional culture and traditions. Norse gods continued to make their presence felt in Swedish folklore as well.

Snorri Sturluson was an important contributor to this revival movement in the 12th century through his skaldic poetry guide called *Prose Edda*. Visual records of Norse mythology are found in picture stones in Gotland. Many visual records include Norse elements as well as Christian elements such as crosses, reflecting an era of the synchronization of Norse Paganism and Christianity.

The Concept of Paganism

It makes sense to understand how the term "paganism" originated and how its meaning has changed over time, considering that we are talking about Norse Paganism. The word "paganism" comes from the Latin root word "paganus," which means civilian, rustic or rural. It was first used in the 4th century C.E. to denote people who followed polytheism. The word was also used for those people whose cultural beliefs included ritual sacrifice.

Paganism in the modern world incorporates practices and beliefs inspired by the ancient world, especially nature worship and animism, and yet it is different from the world's various religions. In the book *A History of Pagan Europe* by Prudence Jones and Nigel Pennick, pagan religions have the following characteristics:

- ***Polytheism*** – Paganism recognizes multiple gods, goddesses, and divine beings.
- ***Nature-Worship*** – Most pagan religions believe in the divinity of nature and worship elements of nature.
- ***Sacred Feminine*** – Another common trait of paganism is the recognition of the female divinity, often referred to as "goddess."

Initially, paganism was used in a derogatory way and implied a sense of inferiority. It was considered to be any religion or belief system followed by rustics and peasants. Slowly, the term began to mean any unfamiliar religion, but in the modern age, the term paganism has changed and has evolved to include new terms as well, such as Polytheistic reconstruction, Neopagan movements, and Modern Paganism.

Chapter 2: The Old Ways – The Vikings and the Anglo-Saxons

Norse Paganism, Vikings, and Anglo-Saxons are closely interconnected. This chapter is focused on the Vikings and the Anglo-Saxons.

Viking Paganism

Vikings are usually seen as barbarians, raiders, and heathens, a perception created by the religious writers of the Medieval Period. But these ideas are slowly changing today, thanks to new archeological discoveries being made. This group of Nordic people had much more to them than this simplistic depiction. The Vikings lived a life of sophistication and had their own set of traditional practices and belief systems. They were excellent warriors too.

Originating from present-day Sweden, Norway, and Denmark, Vikings started migrating toward coastal Europe around the end of the 8th century. They began as small bands of raiders conducting raids on little villages and slowly expanded into large armies consisting of thousands of soldiers, warriors, and fighters. Here are some interesting Viking facts, belief systems they followed, and a few debunked myths too.

Vikings Were Not Unclean Savages – Vikings are often depicted as unclean and barbarous savages. In truth, they were cleaner than most of the other European tribes they conquered. The Vikings loved to take showers, and this fact is interesting considering that at that time, many tribes were disdainful about regular bathing for the sake of cleanliness. Vikings had a special day referred to as "laurdag" where the Viking people took long, elaborate showers and used accessories such as combs for cleaning.

The Vikings Were Excellent Boat Makers and Sailors – The Vikings were highly successful in conquering many regions along the European coast, which reflected their excellent ability to make boats and sail. In all the Viking raids, they used speedy longboats, empowering them to travel at great speeds.

Also, these longboats allowed the Viking conquerors to enter shallow waters and get close to the land, giving them the advantage of swiftly conducted raids similar to hit-and-runs. The Vikings excelled at making these fast longboats that served their purpose well.

Viking Warriors Killed in Battle Went to Valhalla – According to the Vikings, warriors who were killed in battle were not sent to the regular afterlife. They were sent—actually carried by mythical female beings or valkyries—to a special place called Valhalla, in Asgard. Odin looked after these slain warriors, giving them a life of luxury, and prepared them for Ragnarok, the Viking concept of the end of the world.

Vikings Were Family and Community-Oriented – Vikings are shown as being a savage tribe with no family, community, or social laws. This myth has also been busted, since it is now known that the Vikings had an event called the "Thing" (as translated from the Old Norse language). This special event was conducted to keep law and order and settle legal disputes.

Crimes such as theft were settled, and sentences passed on to the parties found guilty, much like the current legal system. The decisions reached in the special event were considered ultimate with no further appeal, and everyone in the tribe, including the powerful people, had to abide by them. Occasionally, women were allowed to attend this event to express their opinions.

The fact that the Vikings played ice sports also speaks to their community-based living. Vikings turned their ice-cold and snowy regions to their advantage by playing multiple snow-based games and sports. Some scholars believe that the Vikings may have been the first to ski and skate on ice. They also played a sport called knattleikr, resembling modern-day ice hockey.

The Concept of Divorce Existed in Viking Society – Women were allowed to participate and express their views during the "Thing" and had multiple privileges and rights, most of which were not part of contemporary European tribes the Vikings conquered. For example, Viking women had property and divorce rights.

If the man didn't run his household and/or farm well and could not provide for his family, the wife could approach the concerned people in power for a divorce. Other reasons for divorce included physical and mental abuse. In fact, divorce was an easy process to follow, as well. The concerned party just needed two witnesses and to state that she was divorcing her spouse. This procedure had to be repeated in two places, one was a public place outside the family home, and the second was within the home near the nuptial bed.

Some of Our Weekdays Are Named after Viking Gods – Many scholars believe that a number of our weekdays are named in honor of Viking gods. For example, Thursday is believed to be an Anglican form of "Thor's Day," the Norse god of thunder and lightning. Scholars also believe that Wednesday is named after Wooden, which is another name for Odin. Tyr inspires Tuesday, and Friday is named after Frigg.

Belief Systems of the Vikings

The Vikings believed in numerous gods and goddesses who were elaborately described in Norse mythology. Vikings were followers of Norse Paganism. There were little, or no written sources or codified texts representing the Old Norse religion during the Viking Age. Along with the belief in a number of gods, goddesses, and divine beings, the Vikings also practiced multiple traditional rituals and rites, especially during special occasions and events to commemorate them.

The most important deities of Norse Mythology included Thor, Odin, Heimdall, Loki, Balder, Tyr, and Frigg. Each of these divine beings was associated with certain elements or things, and each of them had unique functions and powers too. For example, Thor was the god of thunder and lightning.

Vikings believed in two tribes of gods, namely Aesir and Vanir. Odin, Thor, Frigg, Balder, Loki, and others belonged to the Aesir tribe. Odin was the chief god as well as the god of wisdom, death, war, and property. His wife was Frigg, and she was the goddess of marriage and motherhood. Thor, the most powerful among the pantheon of Viking gods, was Odin's son and the god of thunder, lightning, and storms. Loki was considered to be a powerful but unpredictable god who gave birth to many evil beings and creatures.

All the gods and goddesses played important parts and roles in Norse mythology. The various details and stories of the pantheon of gods and goddesses of Norse Paganism are contained in Norse mythology, along with creation myths and conflicts between gods and humans, gods and heroes, and many other tales. According to Norse mythology, our cosmology, consisting of many worlds and realms, is centered on Yggdrasil's cosmic tree.

Rites and Rituals – Vikings believed in and commonly practiced sacrificial rites and rituals. They sacrificed different animals like cows, roosters, hens, and dogs. Even human sacrifice, especially the slaves of Vikings, was a common occurrence in the Viking Age. Human sacrifices took place at specific religious locations and/or temples.

So why and when were sacrifices performed by the Vikings? Sacrificial rituals were performed in honor of various gods and goddesses and on special occasions. For example, sacrifices were conducted before the Viking warriors set out for battle or set out on a journey, especially sea voyages, and even after completing a deal. Also, sacrifices were typical rituals during certain ceremonies such as marriages and funerals.

Marriage Ceremonies Among the Vikings – Marriages were an important aspect of Viking culture and tradition. Often, preparations for marriages would take up to three years because the concerned families needed to settle dowries, property transfers, and inheritances through the marriage. Marriages were grandly celebrated, and festivities could go on from three to seven days.

Friday was considered an auspicious day for marriages because it honored the goddess of marriage. An important event during the marriage was the handing over of the family's sword (usually passed on for generations) by the groom to his bride. She would hold it safely until she could pass it on to their son. In return, the bride passed her father's sword to the groom as a symbol of transferring her guardianship from her father to her husband.

Role of Magic in Norse Mythology and the Viking Culture – Magic was a potent element of the Vikings' belief system. They were predisposed to different forms of superstition. The Vikings believed that Odin discovered the power and wisdom of magic. He is believed to have invoked a volva (a class of powerful Norse witches) to get some questions answered. Interestingly, Norse mythology depicts mostly feminine figures practicing magic, driving the idea that magic was a feminine prerogative.

Temples of the Vikings – Vikings constructed temples for their gods, goddesses, and deities, including Odin and Thor. Often, temples were used for rituals and sacrifices. Numerous large mounds found all over Scandinavia are believed to be sites of Old Norse temples. Also, scholars believe many of the temples were demolished and replaced by churches later. As of today, no Viking temples survive.

Viking Burials – Multiple archeological evidence points to the fact that the Vikings believed in the concept of an afterlife and equipped the dead accordingly. Dead bodies were buried along with many items, including jewelry. Burials were elaborate ceremonies that often included sacrifices as well. Human sacrifices of slaves were often performed because the Vikings believed the slaves would accompany the dead person in the afterlife.

The Decline of Norse Paganism Among the Vikings – When the Vikings started attacking and conquering the European coasts at the end of the 8th century, they were exposed to Christianity. Most of the Vikings that set out to conquer these regions settled in these parts of Europe, including Normandy, Ireland, and Britain. The settlers slowly started accepting and adopting the tenets of the new religion until, eventually, most of them converted to Christianity.

Soon, Christianity spread to Scandinavia too, and by the end of the 12th century, it was firmly established in the Viking strongholds of Sweden, Denmark, and Norway. With the acceptance and increasing popularity of Christianity, Norse Paganism began to decline. Some of the ideas were lost, while others were merged into the new religion.

Anglo-Saxon Paganism

Anglo-Saxon paganism refers to the old belief systems and practices followed by the Anglo-Saxons between the 5th and 8th centuries. Anglo-Saxon paganism, also referred to as Anglo-Saxon traditional religion and Anglo-Saxon pre-Christian religion, consisted of a variety of cultic beliefs and practices from different geographical regions.

Believed to be an Iron Age religion, it was introduced to Britain by the migrating Anglo-Saxons (distinct from Roman-British peoples) from Germanic regions in the mid-5th century. They brought their culture and belief systems to Britain, which remained dominant until Christianity's consolidation around the 8th century.

Our knowledge about the pre-Christian Anglo-Saxon paganism comes to us from textual sources, especially those written by Christian Anglo-Saxons like Aldhelm and Bede. Other sources that build our knowledge of these times are archeological evidence and toponym or place-names. This polytheistic belief system had a central theme of deities referred to asése (singular ós), which was a word for God in Old English.

Place names such as Easole, which translates to God's Ridge (in Kent), and Eisey, which translates to God's Island (in Wiltshire), gives us toponymic evidence of old Anglo-Saxon religion. Woden, or Odin, gets the maximum exposure in this belief system. Examples of Anglo-Saxon paganism through place names include Woodnesborough, which means Woden's Barrow in Kent, Wansdyke or Woden's Dyke in Wiltshire, and Wensley or Woden's Wood in Derbyshire.

Interestingly, Woden comes as an ancestor of Wessex, Kent, and East Anglia's royal lineages. Scholars believe that when Woden lost his divine status as Anglo-Saxon paganism declined, he was adopted as an ancestor in numerous royal families. Some other important gods were Thunor and Tiw. The pre-Christian Anglo-Saxons also believed in a range of supernatural beings like dragons, elves, and Nicor (shape-shifting water creatures).

Thunor is the second most popular deity in Anglo-Saxon paganism. The hammer and the swastika were believed to be this god's symbols representing thunderbolts. These symbols were found in many Anglo-Saxon graves and carved on excavated cremation urns. Place names related to Thunor include Thundersley or Thunder's Woods in Wessex, Thunderfield in Surrey, and Thunores hlaew or Thunor's Mound in Kent. The third important divine figure in Anglo-

Saxon paganism is Tiw, who is identified with the Polaris star, and sometimes is referred to as the god of war.

The most popular female divinity among the pantheon of Anglo-Saxon pagan gods was Frig though there is very little evidence of how and in what role she was worshipped. Some scholars suggest that she might have been the goddess of love and/or festivity. Scholars also believe that her name is associated with place names such as Frethern in Gloucestershire, and Froyle, Freefolk, and Frobury in Hampshire.

Followers of the Anglo-Saxon pagan belief system demonstrated their devotion for their gods and goddesses in various ways, especially by sacrificial rituals, which included sacrificing animals as well as inanimate objects. These special rituals were performed at important religious festivals in temples, evidence of which is seen even today.

Scholars believe that it is likely that most of the cult practices and rituals took place in the outdoors. There is little evidence regarding the afterlife beliefs of Anglo-Saxon pagans, although excavated tombs reveal that the dead were buried or cremated with grave goods. Today, we know of nearly 1200 Anglo-Saxon pagan cemeteries. Both burials and cremations were used in funeral practices. The cremated remains were collected in urns and buried along with grave goods.

Men appear to have been buried with at least one weapon, usually a seax (an Old English word for knife). But some graves revealed more than one weapon, including spears, shields, and swords. Interestingly, non-human animal body parts such as sheep, goats and oxen, were also found, indicating that the funeral customs could have included meats to be buried to serve as food for the deceased on his or her journey to the afterlife.

Anglo-Saxon legends, myths, and other works of literature were transmitted orally, and there is very little evidence of written sources. The only extant Anglo-Saxon epic is the tale of Beowulf. Even scholars regard this surviving text as being recorded by Sepa, a Christian monk. The period when he might have written it is unclear, and most historians believe it could have been written anytime between the 8th and 11th centuries.

Beowulf's story is set in Scandinavia and is based around Beowulf, a Geatish warrior who journeys to Denmark to kill a monster named Grendel. Geats, also referred to as Goths, occupied Gotaland or Geatland (present-day southern Sweden). Beowulf defeats Grendel, who was wreaking havoc on the Hrothgar kingdom and his equally dangerous mother.

According to the story, after the successful slaying of Grendel and his mother, Beowulf becomes the king of Gotaland. He dies when trying to fight off a ferocious dragon. We know this poem has its origins in Anglo-Saxon paganism because of the various pagan beliefs elaborated on within the text, including cremation beliefs. Still, it contains references to biblical figures, which makes it look like the work of a clergyman.

Modern Paganism has adopted various elements of pre-Christian Anglo-Saxon practices, especially in the modern religious movements such as Heathenry and Wicca. Wicca, particularly the Seax-Wicca sect, combines Wiccan and Anglo-Saxon beliefs and deity names.

Chapter 3: Heathenry Vs. Asatru

Heathenry is a new religious movement that is known by multiple other terms, including Heathenism, Germanic Neopaganism, or contemporary Germanic Paganism. It was developed in Europe in the early 20th century and is based on pre-Christian beliefs followed by the Germanic tribes from the Iron Age until the Early Middle Ages.

Heathenry is an attempt to revive and reconstruct ancient belief systems using remaining evidence from folklore, history, and archeology. Heathenry is a polytheistic belief system that focuses on a pantheon of gods, goddesses, and deities from the pre-Christian era of the Germanic regions. The followers of this new religious movement have adopted the cosmological perspectives from ancient societies and tribes. They believe in animism too, or that the cosmos, including the natural world we see around us, are filled with spirits and other divine beings and creatures.

"Heathens," as the followers of Heathenry call themselves, believe in a system of ethics based on loyalty, personal integrity, and honor. Beliefs in the afterlife are varied but this topic does not get much attention among the Heathens.

Practitioners are trying to understand and revive forgotten belief systems by using one or more of the following sources:

- Old Norse texts related to Iceland, including the *Poetic Edda* and *Prose Edda*.
- Old English recordings such as Beowulf.
- German texts of the Middle Ages such as *Nibelungenlied*.
- Archeological evidence that throws light on the pre-Christian age of northern Europe.
- Folklore-based stories and tales collectively referred to as "Lore" by Heathens.

Heathenry believers perform sacrificial rites and rituals referred to as "blots," where a variety of libations and food are offered to their deities. Most of the rituals include a ceremony called symbel, which consists of offering a toast of an alcoholic beverage to the gods. Some practitioners also perform rituals to achieve an altered state of reality through visions and wisdom from the invisible spiritual beings and deities. The most popular of these rituals include the seiðr and galdr.

While some practitioners indulge in these rituals individually, some Heathens perform the ceremonies in little groups called "kindreds" or "hearths." The group rituals are usually conducted in open spaces or in buildings constructed specifically for this purpose.

The Origins and History of Heathenry

Heathenry is a new religious movement (NRM) or a Reconstructionist form of modern Paganism. This movement was developed to revive and get a contemporary understanding of the practices and rituals followed by the pre-Christian traditions and cultures of northern Europe, more specifically, the Germanic cultures.

Heathenry developed during the Romantic era of the 19th and early 20th centuries. During this period, pre-Christian tribes and societies of Germanic Europe gained a lot of popularity. Groups of believers actively worshipped and venerated deities of these ancient tribes of Austria and Germany in the 1900s and 1910s. Nearly all the newly formed belief systems dissolved after World War II.

In the 1970s, new formalized groups and organizations were established and developed in North America and Europe. The issue of race was a central theme in these organizations. The older sects adopted an attitude of racism, referred to as "folkish." These older divisions of Heathenry believed themselves to have ethnic links to a Germanic race, reserved only for white people, and more specifically, only for those with North European roots.

These small divisions within Heathenry combined the belief of racism with right-wing and white supremacist beliefs and perspectives. On the other hand, numerous Heathens had a Universalist approach proclaiming that their religion was open to all and was independent of origin, race, and other discriminatory elements.

The term Heathenry is often used to describe the new religious movement entirely. But there are many groups and sects within this movement, and each of these divisions has its own preferred name, which is based on its ideologies and belief systems. Heathens who believe and follow the Scandinavian sources and belief systems use the terms Ásatrú, Vanatrú, or Forn Sed. Other sects use the following terms/phrases:

- Anglo-Saxon traditions – Theodism or Fyrnsidu.
- German traditions – Irminism.
- Far-right and "folkish" perspectives – Odinism, Folkism, Wodenism, Wotanism, or Odalism.

It is currently believed that there are about 20,000 Heathens globally, with the most active practitioners living in America, Europe, and Australasia. Each of these groups interprets historical sources differently. Some are involved in reconstructing past practices and beliefs accurately.

Some others are open to experimentation and are willing to embrace new interpretations and innovations. And some other groups adopt practices and traditions including their own experiences and personal lessons gained by the experimentations. A few other sects and divisions of Heathenry combine Germanic cultures with ancient surviving practices of other geographies, including Afro-American religions, Hinduism, Buddhism, Taoism, etc.

Understanding Asatru

Asatru is one of the sects of Heathenism. "Tru" literally means "faith" in the Icelandic language, and therefore, Asatru translates to Aesir's faith or belief. As you already know, Aesir were gods from one of the tribes of deities worshipped in Norse Paganism. Asatru practitioners are called Asatruar. The primary focus of Asatru is on the Nordic gods and goddesses of Scandinavia but Asatruars' worship other deity groups, including the Vanir, elves, dwarfs, and valkyries.

Another name for Asatru is Vanatru, or those who venerate the Vanir tribe of Nordic deities. A smaller group of Asatruars venerates and worships the jotnar (or jotunn) and refers to their community as Rokkatru. Forn Sed or the "Old Way" is another common term used to replace Asatru. Most of the right-wing people prefer to call their belief system Odinism, Wodenism, etc.

Understanding Heathenism and Asatru

As you already know by now, Paganism is a collective term including multiple forms of belief systems and traditions, including Celtic Paganism, Slavic Paganism, and even Wicca, and so forth. Heathenism is specifically for Germanic and Nordic gods and deities, including Odin, Thor, Grigg, Friya, and others.

Asatru is a modern Icelandic term that is related specifically to the worship and veneration of the Aesir gods. Asatru is a term that is used often in formal settings among the Asatru community, more often than Norse Paganism or Heathenism. Although followers of Asatru know and believe in the Vanir gods, they don't talk about or worship any other deities but those from the Aesir tribe. Some believe that Vanatru is a direct outcome of the lack of involvement and engagement by the Asatruar with the Vanir deities.

Asatru has a fairly rigid and formalized set of rules to follow. The things that are expected of you as a follower of that faith could lead to a large formal community that follows the belief system. On the other hand, Heathenism and Norse Paganism seek small-scale communities that are self-sufficient in each of their traditions, cultures, and belief systems.

Although the emergence of Heathenism and Asatru are rooted in Norse Paganism, many of the modern Asatruar tend to use the term Asatru because, for the uninitiated, words like Paganism, Norse Paganism, and Heathenism tend to have a negative connotation.

One of the most important things to know about Asatru is that there is no missionary or proselytizing events that happen. People can join the community if they want. There is nothing given in return for becoming a Heathen. You do it only if it is your calling.

The Asatru Association

The Asatru Association is an Icelandic religious formalized organization of Heathenry established on the First Day of Summer in 1972 by Sveinbjörn Beinteinsson, a farmer and poet. The First Day of Summer in Iceland is a national holiday and is celebrated on the first Thursday after April 18th annually. The Asatru Association was recognized and registered as a religious organization in 1973. The chief religious official or the highest office of the Asatru Association is referred to as "Allsherjargodi," an elected post.

The priests in Asatru are called Godi, and each Godi is given a congregation called godord to work with. While each godord is more or less connected to certain geographic regions, there is no compulsion to join any specific godord. You are free to join any congregation that you like.

The legal approval allowed the organization to conduct legally binding rituals and ceremonies as well as to collect a share of the church tax, which is imposed by the tax on religious congregations to run and manage churches and their employees. Sveinbjörn Beinteinsson led this organization from its inception in 1972 until his death in 1993. During his time, the membership of this organization did not exceed 100 people, and there was not much activity.

The second Allsherjargodi was Jörmundur Ingi Hansen, who led the organization from 1994 to 2002, and it was during this time when the Asatru Association witnessed considerable activity and growth. The third and current leader is the musician Hilmar Örn Hilmarsson, who took charge in 2003.

Asatru does not conform to a fixed religion, theology, or dogma. Each individual is free to have his or her own beliefs. For example, many Wiccan members are also members of the Asatru Association. The Asatru priests believe in a pantheistic perspective. The communal blot feast is the central ritual of Asatru. The priests also conduct naming ceremonies called gooar, weddings, funerals, coming of age, and other rituals too.

The Blot Ritual

The communal blot festival is an important occasion in Asatru. The blot starts with hallowing the ritual with a specific formula. Another important element at the start of the blot ritual is the declaration of truce and peace among all the members present there. The chanting of verses from the *Poetic Edda* follows this ceremony. The next stage consists of passing a drinking horn wherein the participants toast and drink in honor of the gods, ancestors, and wights. Libations are also offered to the worshipped deities.

This initial part of the ritual usually happens outdoors, followed by a communal feast that usually takes place indoors. The communal feast is accompanied by entertainment in various forms, including music and dance. There are four annual blot ceremonies, including:

- The Jolablot or the Yuleblot on Winter Solstice - a special event on this day is the lighting of candles by children to celebrate the Sun's rebirth.
- The Sigurblot or the Victory blot on the First Day of Summer.
- The Sumarblot or summer blot on Summer Solstice.
- The Veturnattablot or Winter Night blot on the First Day of Winter.

In addition to these four main blots, other forms of similar rituals for individuals such as gooar and even local blots for smaller communities are conducted. All the rituals and ceremonies of the Asatru Association, including the weekly meetings, are open to the public.

Asatru Perspectives

The modern Asatru/Heathenism community has three primary perspectives, namely, Universalism, Folkism, and Tribalism. Of these three, the first two perspectives are the main ones, while the third, Tribalism, takes a middle-ground approach.

Universalism - According to the people who believe in this perspective, anyone from any background can become a Heathen. A Universalist perspective offers more freedom of choice to everyone, even while giving greater options for Heathenism to grow and expand its reach across the globe.

Therefore, a Universalist will welcome a Japanese person into his or her fold of Asatru as long as the initiate is willing to understand the lore of Norse Paganism, live his or her life based on the nine virtues, learn and understand the runes of Asatru, and take responsibility for his or her own actions. Most importantly, a Universalist values common sense.

One of the primary arguments against Universalism, especially from the Tribalists and Folkish, is that it is very open-ended. People of the other two perspectives believe that there should be a few vital threshold criteria that need to be met before allowing anyone to practice Asatru. Conversely, Universalists believe that these vital criteria are already there, those which have been discussed in the previous paragraph.

Folkism – The Folkish perspective believes that Asatru is an ethnic religion and entry should be restricted only to those with a North European heritage. This belief of Folkism is based on the idea that ethnic religions connect followers to the local landscape, bloodline, ancestors, and traditions. So, outsiders can't find a connection with the ethnic elements and will fail to be genuine practitioners.

Many people accuse those who follow Folkism of being white supremacists because of their rigid approach regarding their entry into Asatru, but the Folkish argue that their stand has nothing to do with white supremacy but is based on the deep belief that every ethnic community must worship its own ancestors.

People who oppose Folkism also use another argument in their favor. They quote the presence of multiple non-Norse people and characters in the Eddas and other Norse folklore and legends. These non-Norse characters took part in rituals and rites too. Also, slaves in the Nordic community came from other lands and regions, including Slavic, Celtic, and even Middle Eastern. And many of these slaves were freed and emancipated by their masters and allowed to settle and live the Nordic life.

On the other hand, the Norse people who migrated to other lands also adopted and absorbed those lands' cultures and traditions. Despite these arguments, Folkism stands firm in its principle to not allow all and sundry into the Asatru fold.

Tribalism - Folkism and Universalism are at the two ends of the Asatru spectrum, while those who follow Tribalism take a middle stand. They accept and embrace the Folkish stand of the need for a deep connection and feeling for Norse culture to be able to call oneself an Asatru. Surface-level adoption of Asatru principles is not enough. A person can be inducted into the clan in one of two ways, specifically if he or she is of Germanic origin or if the person is converted, adopted or takes an oath into the community.

Regardless of the perspective you choose to take, the vital thing is to remember that the Nordic people greatly valued courage, honor, freedom, individuality, growth, and development. Also, those of us who feel a calling to join the path of Asatru will have to experience the belief system only in the current, modern-day scenario. Therefore, being able to practice the Old Norse religion, the way it existed during the Viking Age, is impossible.

The critical thing is that your connection to Asatru must be deep. It calls for a commitment and it should definitely go beyond learning about Odin, Thor, and other deities. Wearing a miniature of Thor's hammer around your neck is not enough. You will have to learn to live the life of a true Norse pagan.

Chapter 4: The Nine Noble Virtues and Other Codes

Now that you have a fairly good idea of the meaning and context of Norse Paganism, Heathenry, and Asatru, it is time to get deeper into what defines the life of an Astruar. A few types of frameworks of codes and value systems govern Asatru. These codes act as guidelines for the followers to lead a life based on Asatru principles. These codes were formed and collated from various sources, including the Icelandic Sagas and the *Poetic Edda*.

The Nine Noble Virtues, also referred to as NNV or 9NV, consist of two sets of ethical and moral situational guidelines. Sir John Yeowell and John Gibbs-Bailey created one set of codes. Sir Yeowell, also known as Stubba, and John Gibbs-Bailey, also known as Hokuld, were members of the Odinic Rite, an international organization dedicated to Odinism and Asatru.

Some believers credit Edred Thorsson with codifying the first set of NNV when he was a member of the Asatru Folk Assembly (AFA). Stephen A. McNallen, a member of the AFA, codified the second set of the NNV. Edred Thorsson and Darban-i-Den were the pen names of Stephen Edred Flowers. Some other sets of Asatru moral and ethical codes include:

- The Nine Charges - discussed in detail in another section of this chapter.
- The Six-Fold Goal - right wisdom, harvest, might, firth, and love.
- The Aesirian Code of Nine - knowledge, honor, protect, change, flourish, conflict, fairness, balance, and control.

The Nine Noble Virtues

Courage

The Asatru defines courage as an element of pagan virtue that drives an individual to act and behave in the right way, even in the absence of reward or in the face of certain defeat. This definition clearly emerged in all the Norse stories and legends. The powerful monsters are central to all Norse mythological themes, but they were not given an honorable character.

Contrarily, the heroes found potent solutions to kill the monsters driven by sheer courage and willpower. In fact, the concept of courage being paramount in a person's life is the reason, however misplaced, that gave rise to the opinions that the Vikings were godless.

The Viking people were so focused on their courage to do the right thing that they believed that martial heroism was a power of its own. In today's world, courage is more than martial bravery. It also means to stand up for the right thing. For example, turning into a whistleblower when the company you work for has violated laws is considered to be a courageous thing to do, according to the Asatru.

Norse Paganism believed that courage was all about having faith and trust in your own strength. Courage, according to Asatru, also includes being brave to live according to the Nine Noble Virtues. Asatruars believe that it is vital to stand up in a hostile world to be counted among the true and authentic people of character.

Courage is:

- Having the conviction and inner strength to face the enormity of the task at hand.
- Standing by your friends and family.
- Keeping alive and following Asatru principles.

From the *Poetic Edda,* Havamal explains courage like this, "The coward believes that he will live forever, if he holds back in the battle, but in old age he shall have no peace, though spears have spared his limbs."

Truth

The truth is to say and do what is right and true. It is the willingness to be straightforward and honest. If you cannot be honest, it is better not to say anything at all. And in the same way, if you have to talk, then it is vital that you speak the truth as you see it and not as what others want to hear. Telling the truth might be painful at times, but it is better to deal with the short-term effects of pain by being truthful rather than lying, which has far more harmful consequences.

Courage and truth are interlinked, because courage fosters and encourages truth, and the reverse is also true. When you build your ability to speak the truth in your life, you also build the courage to face the consequences. Truth is the underlying virtue of holiness, even as it strengthens us toward being courageous. In the absence of truthfulness in your character, you are unlikely to meet with any kind of spiritual realization.

Being courageous and truthful requires persistent efforts. You must incessantly strive to do the right thing and live according to what you know and believe as being true and correct. Truthfulness is a virtue valued by our ancestors. Being truthful also helps you in being modest. You find it easy not to exaggerate your achievements as well as accept your failures with humility.

There is an interesting warning with regard to speaking the truth. Undoubtedly, you must always try to speak the truth, but you must not be naïve enough to talk the truth with people who spout lies to you. According to the Havamal, it might be a good thing to counter lies with lies to guarantee that you are not taken for a ride by the scamsters of the world.

One of the verses about truth explained in Havamal goes as follows, "Do not promise something you cannot live up to. Breaking your word has serious consequences."

Honor

Honor is all about the value of recognizing and accepting nobility, both within and outside of us. Honor is not only your own feeling of self-worth rooted in your noble character, but also showing respect to others. Perhaps honor is one of the most difficult virtues to define because different people can interpret it differently.

The importance of living an honorable life is contained in this small proverb in the *Poetic Edda,* "Everything and everyone in this world dies. However, the reputation of dead people never dies." So, good or bad deeds survive even after our deaths, and they carry the glory or burden of our soul.

Astruars see honor as the value they add to the community. The answers to the following questions can tell you whether honor exists in your personality:

- Are you an upstanding person in your community?

- Do people come to you for help and advice, especially regarding morals and principles?

- Do people trust your word? Or do they always second-guess what you say?

Without honor, we cannot evolve or progress in our lives. Also, dishonorable people tend to hold back the progress of their families and community. Our actions and deeds reflect our honor and our self-worth. Striving to be worthy of the place we occupy in the world, community, and family is all part of an honorable life.

Fidelity

Fidelity is the willingness to be loyal to your faith and belief systems, including the deities, and to your community, friends, and yourself. There are many levels of loyalty, which are individual-specific and situational-specific. Each of us knows and understands the depth of the various levels of loyalty we feel within ourselves.

Fidelity in Asatru includes your commitment:

- To your faith (Asatru).
- To your community and kindred.
- To your family responsibilities.
- To your intention of making the world a better place.

Courage forms the foundation on which loyalty and commitment build their strengths. When we are courageous, we find the power to hold the bonds that tie us to our faith, community, and family. These bonds of togetherness drive us to accept ourselves as a conduit through which progress for the family and community takes place. These bonds of commitment are what weave the tapestry of Asatru.

Interestingly, "troth" is the German word for loyalty and faith. In ancient times, a warrior who survived while his lord died—or failed to die for his tribe or community's safety and protection—was dishonored and shunned by his society.

Fidelity is also about honoring your promises and oaths, including wedding vows. Oaths and promises are sacred contracts, and those who break these contracts are the biggest offenders, according to Asatru NNV.

Generosity and fidelity are connected to each other at a very deep level. Giving is a way to strengthen fidelity. When you are loyal, then you find your ability to be generous and giving also improves. Giving is not only in the form of materialistic things but also in the gift of love, time, etc. Importantly, the act of generosity is not one-sided but has to work both ways. According to ancient Heathens, if you do not return the giver with your own generosity, then you will lose the power of the gift you received.

A passage in Havamal on fidelity goes like this, "If you have a friend you trust, then it is your duty to pray for his goodwill, to exchange gifts and thoughts, and visit his house even as you invite him to your house as often as possible."

Discipline

Discipline, or self-discipline, is your ability to be hard on yourself to improve your life. Once you are disciplined, then you should try to help others in need toward their self-development. As the concept of discipline and self-development spreads in the community, the entire tribe or clan progresses and great purposes are achieved.

The lesson of discipline should not be taught through words, but through actions. It is easy to tell others to do what you say and not do what you do. Even so, Asatru does not approve of this approach. You will have to lead by example. It calls for an enormous amount of willpower and discipline to stay on the difficult path of Asatru instead of choosing another potentially easier path. Only when you stay on your path of commitment will others follow suit.

Discipline and fidelity work in tandem. Discipline provides the willpower to be loyal, and fidelity, in turn, motivates you to be disciplined and be true and committed to your values and principles. These two virtues help us shape our worth and destiny. Havamal describes discipline in the following way, "A person who rises early, keeps few slaves, does his own work rises in his life and earns wealth and prosperity. A person who sleeps late loses a lot in his life."

Hospitality

Hospitality is the sense of service you have. It reflects your willingness to share what you have with your people and community. Of course, this does not mean that you mindlessly give away everything you have to anyone who comes knocking at your door. Hospitality is about sharing and giving and has a reciprocity effect as well.

When guests come to your house, it is your duty to make them as comfortable as you can, and to offer them food and drink. Hospitality is a very important virtue in Asatru: their gods travel all over the cosmos, including to Midgard or the realm of human beings. With that in mind, a guest in your house could be a god in disguise, and it is your duty to honor him or her.

Also, hospitality drives a sense of readiness to help and assist people in need. It drives interdependence in the community and forges strong bonds among the members. In fact, for ancestors, hospitality was not just a virtue, it was a necessity. In those days, traveling long distances posed a lot of difficulties and was also dangerous. Yet, traveling was important for trade and commerce. So, Norsemen and women of those times freely opened their homes not only to their friends and other known tribespeople but also to strangers.

People who came knocking would be provided with a warm place to rest their tired feet, warm food to fill their bellies, and even warm clothes to wear. In return, the guest was expected to eat moderately, entertain their hosts with songs and stories, and give little gifts such as small trinkets. Havamal talks about the importance of hospitality in the following way: "A guest who has traveled needs the warmth of a fire for his numb knees, warm water to wash, clean clothes and food to fend off the hunger and cold."

Self-Reliance

This virtue reflects your spirit of independence. When you are self-reliant, you are independent for yourself and empower your family toward this virtue. It is important to remember that being self-reliant does not mean you should deny your interconnectedness with others. It is about having the ability to first take care of yourself, and then work toward helping others in need. Self-reliance helps you to provide food to eat for yourself as well as share what you have with others in need.

Self-reliance teaches you to find solutions for your problems. It teaches you to build skills to make your life better than it is today. It teaches you not to waste time and to use your skills effectively to learn new things so that you can bring prosperity to your life.

Self-reliance is a vital element of freedom. When you are self-reliant, you are free to make your own decisions. You can think for yourself and find solutions that suit you best. When you taste freedom, you earn more freedom, and you become increasingly self-reliant. Self-reliance is about using your own wisdom and intellect to understand yourself and the world around you.

Industriousness

This virtue is all about your willingness to work hard at all times and to strive for efficiency. The trick is in seeing the journey of industriousness as a joyous activity. It is imperative that we work hard to achieve our goals, to find what we seek. Without hard work and perseverance, we can never reach our goals.

And yet, working hard without time to relax and enjoy your life is also not the Asatru way. Industriousness is a virtue that has hard work at its core, but it also means you take pride in your work. Asatru's definition of industriousness goes a little above and beyond too. The value system of Asatru says this about industriousness: "Unless you are disabled, a full-time student, or already employed, it is your duty to find a job and do it diligently."

If you have a problem finding a job, then endeavor to find some like-minded people and start a venture. Asatruars believe that without work, there can be no self-worth. We cannot provide for our families. We cannot achieve our goals or strive to reach perfection in our lives. Being lazy is one of the worst lessons you can teach your children.

Industriousness also means striving hard for self-improvement. We should not be happy with mediocrity or working in a way that simply helps us to survive. Our industriousness should drive us to achieve greater efficiency and productivity and to thrive in our lives. This virtue is specifically useful in the modern era where life has become very convenient. It is easy to go to a grocery store, come home, put some ingredients together, and create a meal for yourself, unlike the ancient times when there was a lot of work to do, such as cows to milk, fields to till, cattle to feed, and much more, before food was ready to be eaten. Thus, industriousness was a necessity to prevent starvation.

Today, laziness may not result in starvation, but it does cause a lot of other problems, including joblessness and a total loss of self-worth, without which your life can be a living hell. Self-reliance and industriousness work hand in hand. Your sense of independence will drive you to do your work without depending on anyone. This approach drives you to work hard. You don't wait for things to be done by others, and you don't wait for your life to be handed over to you on a platter.

Perseverance

Perseverance is a virtue that empowers one to stand up and try again despite repeated failures. It is your ability to return stronger after every setback you encounter. It is your ability to stay on the path of your life's purpose until you achieve it. Perseverance is about not giving up until you succeed. Hard work and perseverance are essential elements for success. As an Asatruar, it is your duty to persevere because perseverance is vital for survival. It is a dynamic part of nature. If we don't persevere, we will stagnate and die.

These Nine Noble Virtues form the structural framework of the Asatru community. The members are encouraged to remember and implement each of these ethics so that they can lead a fulfilling, meaningful life, even as they bring happiness to their families and community.

The Nine Charges

The Odinic Rite established the Nine Charges in the 1970s. These nine codes of Asatru ethics and morals are as follows:

1. To maintain honesty and loyalty to a trusted friend; even if he or she hits me, I will not strike back.

2. Never make false promises because the outcome of broken promises is huge and grim.

3. To be gentle with the poor and humble.

4. To respect the elderly and the wise.

5. To fight against all evils and foes of the faith, family, and community.

6. To return friendliness but not to give in to the promise of an untried and untested stranger.

7. Not to give in to the foolish words of a drunken man.

8. To respect and listen to the wise words of our ancestors.

9. To abide by the rules set by lawful authority.

Chapter 5: The Aesir, Vanir, and Jotnar

This chapter is dedicated to the pantheon of Norse gods, goddesses, and other divine beings. Many of the Asatruars seek guidance and help from these deities, but it is important to know that not all practitioners worship or pray to the gods. Instead, followers may seek clarity and guidance to solve problems and lead a meaningful, fulfilling life.

Creation Myth of Norse Mythology

According to Norse Paganism, before the start of time, there was a bottomless abyss referred to as Ginnungagap. This abyss separated the fiery land of Muspelheim and the icy lands of Niflheim. The two realms became powerful and strong and clashed against each other. The fire from Muspelheim thawed the ice in Niflheim and turned it to water drops, which held the potential for life.

The first living being, according to Norse Mythology, was Ymir. Ymir was a hermaphrodite giant who was created from the life-giving water drops. Ymir created children from his armpits as well as rubbed his two legs together, which gave rise to the jotnar, giant, and many other races. Although all the races were born of the same parent, a lot of animosities grew among races, and after a few generations, there was continuous discord among them.

Ymir's descendants were Odin, Vili, and Ve, who together killed Ymir. Then they used Ymir's bones, blood, teeth, eyelashes, hair, skull, and brain to create the Nordic world. The dome of Ymir's skull became the sky that arched over the earth. His blood became the waters of the lakes, rivers, and seas. His brain became clouds. His bones were transformed into hills and mountains, and his hair became trees.

The gods then created a protective fence out of Ymir's eyelashes to separate Jotunheimer, the giant's realm, from what was going to become the Midgard or the human realm. The gods then took over the job of overseeing this border they created to provide safety to the human world.

Norse gods are primarily divided into two categories, the Aesir and Vanir.

The Aesir and Vanir

The Vanir – Historically, the Vanir, a tribe of farmers (worshipped later as ancient powerful gods), are believed to have come to Scandinavia and other parts of northern Europe about 5000 years ago. They brought the gift and power of agriculture, which is why they are considered farmer gods and goddesses. They came to this area after the flooding of the Black Sea.

Considering they were farmers, the Vanir gods are known for their connection to fertility. The important Vanir gods are Njord, Freya, and Freyr. Other deities include the Earth, Night, Day, Sun, and Moon. Day was believed to be the child of Night. Sun was female, and Moon was male.

The Aesir - Historically, the Aesir could have been male warriors who rode on horses and chariots. They are believed to have come from the East during the Indo-European invasions, which took place more than 1000 years after the entry of the Vanir. The Aesir warriors are believed to have wiped out most of the farmers or Vanirs (who were already living in Scandinavia); they retained the culture of the Vanirs and merged it with their own.

The most important Aesir gods were Odin, Frigg, Thor, and Tyr. According to Norse Paganism, half the warriors that die in battle are taken to Valhalla, a great hall in Asgard where Odin rules. The remaining slain warriors are taken to Folkvang (by Freya, the Vanir god), which is ruled by the Valkyries. The Vanirs and Aesirs are believed to have coexisted because the two groups, despite their antagonism, were required to combine their powers in order to prosper.

Norse Deities

Let us look at some gods and goddesses of Norse mythology and how they interacted with each other and with human beings too.

Odin

Odin was the supreme deity in Norse Mythology. He was the greatest and the most revered immortal among Norse gods and was the father of the Aesir tribe. Odin was an awe-inspiring figure who ruled over Asgard. He was not only the god of war but also the god of poetry and magic. His famous possessions are his horse Sleipnir, and his ring, Draupnir.

He is known by many other names, including Wotan and Wodan or Woden. Odin translates to "Master of Fury." He is also the most mysterious and complex god in the pantheon of Norse gods and goddesses.

But above all, Odin's primary trait was an unrelenting quest for knowledge and wisdom. His search for wisdom was not peaceful or serene, but one of continuous activity. His might is compared to the power of a relentless storm, which is never still until it completes its phase of destruction. In the same way, Odin's search for wisdom and knowledge is filled with activities and adventures.

He had two wolves, two ravens, and the Valkyries to help him in his quest. His quest for knowledge was so deep that he willingly sacrificed one of his eyes so that he could see the cosmos more clearly than before. Also, he hung from the World Tree or Yggdrasil for nine days and nights. This perseverance brought him the knowledge of the runic alphabet. He sought knowledge relentlessly, and this attitude helped him to unlock many of the secrets and mysteries of the cosmos.

Interestingly, Odin was not pure at heart, even if he was a god or the king of gods. He is often portrayed as being punished for unfairness and not respecting law and convention. Odin was the god of rulers as well as outlaws. Adam of Bremen, an 11th-century historian, describes Odin's character excellently in the following words: "When Odin was among friends, he made everyone happy with his magic and poetry. When he was at war, the enemies would run helter-skelter at this terrifyingly grim demeanor."

Frigg and Freya

Frigg was Odin's wife and the mighty queen of Asgard. She was the only goddess who had the power and position to sit next to her husband. She was a paragon of love, beauty, fate, and fertility. This powerful Norse goddess had the power of divination, but a blanket of secrecy surrounded her.

Despite her powerful position among the Norse gods, Frigg gets very little mention in the surviving sources of Norse mythology. Her characteristics appear to be combined with those of Freya, the goddess from the Vanir tribes, which, perhaps, reflects the mutual evolution of a friendship between the two tribes.

Freya is such a pleasure seeker that she is considered equivalent to the modern "party girl." In fact, Loki accuses her of sleeping with all the gods, elves, dwarfs, and her own brother too. Despite that, she was much more than just a pleasure-seeker. A highly protective mother, she coerced an oath from all the elements of nature, beasts, poisons, and weapons that they will not harm or kill Balder, her loving and brilliant son.

Freya was a passionate and sensual Norse goddess who was associated with beauty, love, and fertility, similar qualities connected to Frigg. Both Frigg and Freya are depicted as a volva, a female magician of Norse Paganism. They work with a particular form of magic called seidr, which involves deciding destinies as well as bringing about positive changes in the system. Both Frigg and Freya used falcon feathers to shapeshift into the bird.

Freya is deeply connected with seidr, a form of magic and shamanism that works to bring about positive changes in the world and cosmos. The power of seidr is spoken of in glowing terms in Norse mythology. With the magic of seidr in her hand, a powerful magician like Freya could weave new events and personal experiences into a being.

In the Viking age, a volva was deemed to be a sorceress who traveled from place to place to perform seidr magic on commission. She would be compensated for her magic work with food, clothing, and accommodation. A volva was looked upon with a mixture of awe, fear, longing, and idolization.

Balder

Balder was the son of Odin and Frigg. In Norse Mythology, Balder is described as living between heaven and Earth. He was handsome, radiant, kind, and a fair god. Although he was an immortal god, he was killed by deceit with mistletoe, an element that contained his life as well as his death.

Balder was loved by all gods, goddesses, and the jotnar because of his great looks and cheerful and gracious nature. When Balder began to have dreams about his death, Frigg went around to all the elements and beings in the cosmos and secured oaths from all of them not to hurt or kill Balder.

Once this was done, the gods amused themselves by throwing things at him and seeing him unhurt by anything. His mother made one small mistake. She left out the mistletoe from her oath list because she thought it was too small to cause any harm to her son. Loki knew about this, and with the intention of creating harmless mischief, he gave Hod (or Hodr, the blind god) a sprig of mistletoe and asked him to throw it at Balder, as the other gods were doing. When this small mistletoe touched Balder's body, he fell dead.

Loki

This mischievous god was a shapeshifter too. He could transform into many animal forms. Traditionally, Loki is described as being a wight of fire. The fire elements are represented in the description of his traits as an indispensable companion, a deadly master, and an untrustworthy servant. Loki was a tricky god, capable of creating a lot of mischief.

The gifts that Loki could confer on people are believed to be speech, hearing, sight, and appearance. Loki is shown as indulging in double-agent behavior, often betraying one side in favor of another. He creates trouble for the gods and goddesses and finds it delightful to play pranks, including malicious ones. So, while he is known to bring trouble to the gods, he has also been known to rescue them in times of need. Loki is the one who brought the gods many of their famous possessions, including Odin's horse Sleipnir and his ring Draupnir and Thor's hammer, Mjolnir.

As previously mentioned, Loki placed a branch of mistletoe in the hands of Hod, a blind god, and fooled him into throwing it at Balder, instantly killing the son of Frigg and Odin.

Thor

Thor was the most popular and famous son of Odin, and his mother was Earth. He was the protector of the human race and realm. He was also the god of thunder and wielded a powerful hammer called Mjolnir. Thor was famous for his strength, bravery, righteousness, and great healing powers. Another name of Thor is Thunar.

He inherited the powers of storm, wind, and air from his father, Odin. Thor was a warrior god par excellence. He was the ideal god that every human warrior strived hard to emulate. He is the invincible protector of the Aesir clan, as well as their realm, Asgard. His courage and sense of commitment and duty were unparalleled and unshakeable. His strength doubles when he wears his special belt, called Megingjard, which was a gift from his mother.

Thor's most famous weapon is his hammer, the Mjolnir, and he goes nowhere without it. For the Asatruars, Thor embodies thunder, and his hammer embodies lightning. Thor's biggest rival is Jormungand, the great serpent that lies curled around the Earth. In Ragnarok, Thor is believed to die at the hands of this great snake. Thor's wife was Sif, whose famous golden hair made her the protector of yellow ready-to-harvest cornfields.

Freyr

Freyr was an important Vanir clan god who was respected and revered highly. He was the god of prosperity and controlled the weather conditions. Freyr was often depicted with a phallus. Freyr is worshipped as the "foremost of the gods." No one hated him, thanks to his ability to confer wealth and prosperity on people who made him happy.

He is often represented as ecological and sexual prowess, including the health and wellbeing of an individual, peace, wealth, bountiful harvests, etc. In addition to his erect, enormous phallus, Freyr is also depicted with his boar, Gullinborsti, translated to the "one with the golden bristles."

Heimdall

Heimdall was famous for his "white skin" and was considered to be the "shiniest" of all the Norse deities. He was one of Odin's sons. He protected Asgard against attacks and invasions and sat on top of Bifrost, a divine rainbow bridge that connected Midgard, the human realm, to Asgard, the realm of the gods.

Heimdall's home is called Himinbjorg or the Sky Cliffs, on top of the Bifrost. He hardly needs sleep and therefore, is the best guard for Asgard. His eyesight is so sharp that he can see things within hundreds of miles, both during the day and by night. His hearing is so powerful that he can hear wool growing on a sheep's body and the grass growing out of the ground. His horn, Gjallarhorn or Resounding Horn, raises the alarm when he sees danger approaching Asgard.

Hel

Hel was a Norse goddess who ruled over the Norse underworld, Helheim, which was also referred to as Hel. Appearing death-like with pale skin, she nurtured and accommodated anyone who entered her realm. The meaning of her name and her realm is "hidden."

Hel was the daughter of Loki and Angrboda, a giantess. This goddess is depicted as being harsh, cruel, and greedy. At her best, she is indifferent to both the living and the dead. Her most significant appearance in Norse mythology is when Balder dies. Hermod was sent as an emissary to Hel to try to persuade the goddess to return Balder because every living being was crying at his death. But Hel refused to give up Balder easily.

She placed a very harsh condition for his return. She said that if every last element in the cosmos shed a tear for Balder, then she would release him back to the land of the living. Hermod and the other gods got together and made sure every little item in the cosmos cried for Balder, except one giantess. For that one refusal to cry, Hel's terms were not met, and she didn't return Balder, and he remained dead.

Vidar

Vidar was the son of Odin and a giantess, Grid. His powers were equal to that of Thor. Though, he makes an appearance in only one place in Ragnarok. Vidar translates to "the wide-ruling one." Vidar was believed to have survived the cataclysmic end of the world, Ragnarok. Vidar survived the end of the world, thanks to a pair of shoes especially crafted for the event.

These magical shoes were made with magical powers. Vidar was able to beat Wolf Fenrir (the one who killed Odin) and not only avenge his father's death but also end the rampage of the evil animal. Although he is as powerful as Thor, he is known as a silent god, and nothing more other than his encounters at Ragnarok are mentioned in the various Norse mythological tales.

Vale

Another son of Odin, Vale (sometimes spelled as Vali) avenged the death of his brother, Balder, by killing the blind god, Hod, who had killed Balder with mistletoe, although under false pretenses given by Loki. His mother was the giantess Rindr. Vale is another survivor of Ragnarok.

Jotnar

Jotnar is the plural of jotunn, a Norse word for a type of divine being distinct from Norse gods and goddesses. Jotnar are defined with different terms and phrases, including thurs, risi, and troll. The term giant is often used as a synonym for jotunn. Yet, jotnar are not necessarily gigantic in size and form. Jotnar can range from alarmingly grotesque to exceedingly beautiful beings. Odin is believed to be a descendant of the jotnar, while other Norse deities such as Geror and Skadi are described as being jotnar.

The gods came later in the Norse creation myth. The jotnar were one of the first beings produced through the hermaphroditic powers of Ymir. They grew from sexless reproduction from certain parts of Ymir's body. The different beings from Ymir's sexless production intermingled with each other and also with the first god, Buri, who appeared in the cosmos. Buri married a jotunn named Bestla.

The jotnar are believed to have survived Ymir's death by sailing to safety through the flood caused by Ymir's blood. The jotnar are believed to reside in Jotunheimen. Negative connotations about the jotnar were rooted in the later versions of Scandinavian folklore. There is hardly a Norse tale without the presence of a jotunn, and the jotnar are presented as one of the prime antagonists, but they were also spouses, friends, parents, and grandparents of the Aesir and Vanir deities.

Loki - Loki was the most famous jotunn. He was the son of Farbauti and Laufey of the jotnar race. Loki was adopted and accepted into the Aesir tribe of gods and became Thor's friend and companion. Even so, he was known as a duplicitous character that could be as mischievous and trouble causing as he was capable of doing a lot of good.

Skadi - The goddess of winter seasons, including its elements such as ice, snow, skiing, hunting, and archery, Skadi was the daughter of Pjazi, the storm god. She is mentioned in various Norse mythology texts, including the *Prose Edda*, the *Poetic Edda*, *Heimskringla*, and also in multiple skaldic poems. She argued and won reparations for her slain father in three different ways:

- She got Odin to place her father's eyes like two stars in the night sky.

- She wanted the gods to make her laugh, but no one was successful at this until Loki managed to make the giantess laugh out loud in happiness.

- She got the gods to agree to let her choose one of the gods to marry. Interestingly, she wanted to choose by looking at their feet. Her intention was to marry Balder, the god of beauty, and she put forth this condition thinking that it would be easy to simply choose him by looking at his beautiful feet. Surprisingly, she ended up choosing Njord, the god of the sea.

Another important being of the jotnar race is Pjazi, Skadi's father, who kidnapped the goddess Idunn, helped by Loki. Goddess Idunn is associated with apples because she was the keeper of a wooden box made of ash wood called Eski, in which she kept special apples. The Eski is used to keep treasured personal possessions. These apples were special because as the gods grew old, they would bite into one of the fruits and regain their youth again.

Loki is forced to kidnap Idunn by Pjazi. The two of them lure the goddess into the forest area, and there, Pjazi takes the shape of an eagle and flies away with Idunn. Then, during the battle with the Aesir gods for her retrieval, Pjazi is killed, for which Skadi makes the gods pay in three different ways, as discussed above. In another story, King Utkarda-Loki, the ruler of Jotunheimer, battles Thor. Another jotunn Hrungir battles Thor too in one of the fiercest battles of Norse mythology.

The jotnar are associated with the elemental forces and the natural world of human beings. The chaotic and destructive energies of nature were dangerous for our ancestors, and so, it is easy to understand why the beings representing these powers are portrayed as antagonists and villains. Even so, many realms of nature were useful for humankind, whose energies were represented as friendly jotnar. For example, Aegir was the giant of the sea and a friend of the gods. He is depicted as hosting grand banquets for his friends from the realm of gods.

Therefore, the jotnar, like all beings of the cosmos, were neither evil nor good in their entirety. They did their best to survive and thrive in their lives, as did the gods of the Aesir and Vanir clans.

Ragnarok

According to Norse mythology, Ragnarok is the cataclysmic destruction of the entire cosmos. For the Vikings and followers of Norse Paganism, Ragnarok was a prophecy of disaster set to happen at an unknown and unspecified time in the future. This concept had an impactful effect on how Vikings lead their lives.

Ragnarok translates to "Fate of the Gods." This event will take place whenever the Norns, the spinners of fate, decide. Ragnarok will be a period of Great Winter, with biting cold winds and snow hitting the cosmos from all directions. The Sun's warmth will not come through at all, and the Earth will be plunged into unprecedented winters, which will last for more than three times longer than the normal winters.

Humankind will have no food, and survival will be at stake. It will be a period of continuous warfare as survival instincts take hold, driving brothers against brothers. Yggdrasil, the World Tree, will tremble. The stars will disappear. Fenrir, the monstrous wolf, and Jormungand, the mighty serpent, will be free from their chains and wreak havoc in the cosmos.

The gods will arm themselves and go to battle, despite knowing the horrible outcome of Ragnarok. The warriors who were preparing at Valhalla will join the battle and fight valiantly, but to no avail. After a slew of destructive battles with all the gods and everything in the cosmos destroyed and killed, the remains of the world will sink into the sea, and nothing but a void will be left.

While some believe this is the end of the tale, others believe that life will arise from this void, and a new and beautiful world will be created.

Even today, the richness and power of Norse mythology continues to haunt and mesmerize people across the globe, regardless of age, race, gender, etc. Replete with numerous sagas, reading and learning Norse mythology can unleash your imagination, transporting you to a world of excitement, adventure, and intrigue.

Chapter 6: Asatru and Nature

Nature is an important aspect of Asatru belief. Land spirits and nature spirits are inextricable elements of Asatru. This chapter is dedicated to this aspect of Norse Paganism.

Unraveling the Vaettir

The word vaettir comes from the Old Norse language and literally translates to "supernatural being." Vaettir, or wights, are nature spirits in Norse Paganism. Vaettir is primarily used to refer to a supernatural being such as landvaettir or land spirits. The word is also used to refer to any supernatural being in the cosmos, including the elves, dwarfs, and even the Aesir and Vanir gods.

Nature spirits are categorized into different families, the prominent ones being the Alfar (or elves) and the Dvergar (or dwarfs). The families often intermarried among themselves as well as with human beings.

Sjo vaettir (or sea spirits) and vatna vaettir (or water spirits) were the guardians and protectors of specific areas of water. For example, there would be a vatna vaettir for a lake or a river, and there would be a dedicated sjo vaettir for a sea or ocean.

Hus vaettir (or house spirits) were guardians of specific households. An example of a hus vaettir is the Swedish Tomte, a solitary nature spirit that guarded a farmstead. It was seen as benevolent and helpful most of the time. An illvatte, on the other hand, is a highly mischievous vaettir and can cause a lot of harm if it is angry or displeased.

Landvaettir (or land spirits) are protectors and guardians of specific grounds such as forest areas (referred to as skovaettir) and farms. When traveling and approaching an unknown land or forest area, Vikings were known to remove their headgear (usually made of carved dragon heads) so as not to frighten the land spirits and provoke them to attack the Vikings needlessly. In fact, the Vikings believed that they would incur bad luck from landvaettir.

Even today, the Icelandic people celebrate and show gratitude for the supernatural spirits who protect and safeguard their island. In fact, the Icelandic coat-of-arms has four land spirits designed on it. These four include a troll-eagle, a troll-bull, a handsome giant, and a dragon.

According to Norse mythology, troll-animals are the jotnar who have shapeshifted into the chosen animal's form and mental attitude. It is believed that these troll animals are very powerful and strong.

Wights in Scandinavian Folklore

According to Scandinavian folklore, wights are believed to look like ordinary human beings and live in underground societies. Like human beings, wights come in different shapes and sizes; they are beautiful and ugly, tall and short. Some sources of Scandinavian folklore highlight the ability of the wights to change shape and size, and even become invisible. They can transform themselves from little creatures to the size of human beings. They wear dresses similar to us too.

Just like humans, wights also take their cattle to graze. Some sources talk about bears being the pig-equivalent for wights, and elks are to them what oxen are to us. Wights usually live harmoniously in the human world, but they can hurt us or create problems for us if we do something they don't like, or if we hurt them or treat them badly.

Wights are guardians of the environment they live in. Wights living in forests are guardians of the forest, those living in and near lakes protect the waters and creatures of the lake, and those living in hills and mountains are guardians of the natural elements of that place. The wights will punish anyone infringing on these spaces.

Wights can also live under buildings and houses. If these places are not managed well, then usually the wights move away from that place. The punitive measures taken by wights against those who infringe, damage, or hurt them or their spaces include:

- Bad luck through animals.
- Diseases and other health issues.
- Causing poverty.

Sometimes, wights can take revenge by sucking on the fingers and toes of the children of the people who created disturbances until the children cry out in pain. The intensity of their punishments depends on the extent of damage and pain we give them, wittingly or otherwise. For example, if we destroy their homes, then they can do the same to our homes. They can set fire to our houses, destroy things, and even kill the people living in the houses.

In Iceland, it is common to consult a wight expert before building a house or even before building infrastructure such as roads and bridges. In fact, there are reports of unexplained road accidents in some parts of Sweden and Iceland, which are attributed to wights. For that reason, it is imperative that you follow certain rules and regulations when it comes to dealing with wights and their spaces. Some of these rules include:

- When walking on forest paths, it is important that you don't walk in the middle of the road because it is believed that the underground wights use this part of the path. Considering they are invisible to human beings, not following this rule of conduct can cause accidents and harm the wights, making them angry and vengeful. The wights tend to take revenge by destroying homes, buildings, tools, and other human elements of the people living in that area. They could also cause illness.

- Before you pour water outside, especially hot water, you should shout, "Watch out!" so that wights can move out of the way and not get drenched. If you don't do this, then the wights are likely to punish you with accidents or health problems.

- Anything that ends up on the floor or the ground belongs to the wights. So, it is vital that what has been dropped is not cleaned up immediately. You must give the wights time to take what they want and clean up only that which they have left behind.

If the wights are happy with your gifts, they reward you well. You could get prosperity, wealth, great partnerships, and relationships, and your health problems could also get solved. Sometimes, wights reward their well-wishers and those who keep them happy with gems and precious stones as well. Initially, the gift you receive may not look great, but it is important to take care of it because it could transform into something beautiful and invaluable overnight.

- The water that was used for bathing and cleaning young, unbaptized children should be disposed of with care. Old beliefs mention that this water should be thrown out only after hot coals are put in it. Also, the clothes of these children should not be hung outside to dry after sunset. If these rules are not followed correctly, then the wights could come and kidnap the children.

- You can contact wights and other supernatural beings if you wish, but you must not try to contact them for selfish reasons. You can do so to give them a gift or to simply stay in touch. Wights will decide if they want to help you only when they see how truly unselfish you are. Remember that wights don't know or care about your needs and desires. They don't like being treated like servants too. They will help you only when they want to, and they know and believe you deserve their help.

  When you are trying to contact the wights, choose a time when the sunlight is not too bright or where electric lights are not too glaring. Wights don't like bright sunlight or electric light. Also, remember not to leave any trash behind.

There are multiple stories about wights causing harm to human beings, including picking up children in anger or taking revenge. Wights are also known for taking adults. While some children and adults were returned after a while, there are many tales where they disappeared for good and never returned.

There are many mysterious tales of farmers being taken by wights to show the farmers how the cattle's droppings fell on their beds and food because the barn was built over the underground house of wights. In many cases, the farmers have moved the barn to a different place, to make sure the wights are not disturbed.

Another interesting story about wights is related to how they need a woman to do the job of a midwife in their world. The popular story among the Nordic people goes something like this: a woman was working in a barn when a strange man came running to her and worriedly asked her to help his wife. The strange man took the barn-worker through a door she had never seen before. They stepped into a beautiful home where a woman was in labor. The woman from the barn helped the pregnant lady give birth to her baby, wrapping up the child to keep it warm. After she stepped back out of the door, the barn-woman turned to see the door had disappeared completely, like it never existed. The next morning, the midwife found a big pile of silver spoons on her table. It was a gift of gratitude from the wights.

Stories abound of wights attending parties in the homes of human beings. They would come in hundreds, bring large amounts of food and drink with them, and leave without a trace when the party was over. However, there are also stories of wights being quite troublesome and not leaving when the party finished. Getting rid of these guests proved to be tricky. Stories of how such pesky wights would leave only when the names of Christian gods were uttered are plentiful in parts of Scandinavia.

Love stories between wights and humans also abound among the Asatru and Norse Pagan community. Sometimes, these love stories end happily with the human or the wight embracing and adopting his or her new home and identity. In some cases, the love stories end in tragedy and abandonment when one of the partners realizes that they are not of the same race as his or her love.

"The Wisdom of Odin" is a YouTube channel run by a follower of Norse Paganism named Jacob. He talks about his experiences with landvaettir and how he has befriended some of them. According to some believers of Norse Paganism, land spirits are there where gods cannot be. So, in some places where you cannot access pagan gods, you can access the land spirits and seek help if you need it.

Land spirits are tied to the land or place they live in, whereas the gods' control is vast. Land spirits are, therefore, handy and help to solve local problems. Land spirits open up channels through which we can connect with nature. Believers tend to make offerings to landvaettir in the form of fruit and vegetables. This ritual is symbolic of showing gratitude to nature for allowing us to access her abundance.

Because of this, such stories about wights thrive in Scandinavian folklore. Today, these stories are taken quite seriously and used as lessons not to harm or destroy nature. The philosophical connection between these folk tales and the power of nature is easy to see. The anger of the river when we abuse her power can be seen when she is flooding. Her destructive abilities can cause a lot of damage to human property and life, and it is her way of getting back at ruthless human beings who are insensitive to the importance of treating nature with respect and dignity.

Also, landslides and other natural disasters in places where humans excessively use natural resources are apparently further proof that wights who protect these elements of nature are angry with human beings and want to take revenge. When you treat nature with respect, she rewards you with abundance by allowing you to use her timber, agricultural produce, and other elements to prosper and be happy in your life.

Stories of wights are not just mythical tales, they also carry vital lessons in humility and dignity for us human beings. Asatru's Nine Noble Virtues embody many of these life lessons taught to us by wights.

Vaettir are seen as friendly beings that are placed by the gods to look after the regions they live in and protect the areas used by human beings. These beings guard and bless the endeavors of human beings, including farming, fishing, hunting, etc., as long as we do not give in to greed and willfully misuse the power of nature.

Other Nature Spirits

Elves - Elves were very important nature spirits for the Germanic people in the pre-Christian era. The popular version that elves are tricky and demonic beings is not really true. They are associated with goddess Freya and the seidr magic that she practices.

Alfar - In Heathenry, this term refers to the male ancestral lineage, but this Old Norse word literally translates to "elf." The Alfar finds mention in Sigvatr Thordarson's poem, "Austrfaravisur," in which he describes the Alfablot, a sacrificial ritual prevalent in ancient Sweden wherein strangers who visit farmsteads are sacrificed to the gods.

Also, Snorri Sturluson speaks of many kinds of elves, such as Dokkalfar, Svartalfar, and Ljossalfar in his work *Prose Edda*. Today, most Heathens believe that Alfar could be the spirits of our dead ancient ancestors who have been buried under the Earth for so long that they have become spirits.

Dwarfs - Dwarfs are frequently spoken of as being synonymous with Dokkalfar and Svartalfar. They are considered to be highly skilled in craftsmanship. They are credited with crafting many important items that are owned and used extensively by the gods and goddesses. In the *Prose Edda*, four dwarfs represent the four cardinal directions and are responsible for holding up the sky in place.

Interestingly, none of the authentic Norse mythological tales describe dwarfs as being ugly and squatty, the most popular depiction of dwarfs. They are described the same as elves are described in these Old Norse stories.

In summary, land spirits live in particular places and/or in some land features like rivers, hills, and mountains. They influence the wellbeing of the land that they rule over and have the power to curse or bless the people who live in that particular place or depend on that piece of land for anything. They are fierce protectors of the land they dwell in and are quite intolerant toward people who abuse or disrespect nature.

Chapter 7: Yggdrasil and the Nine Worlds

The cosmology of Asatru revolves around the World Tree referred to as Yggdrasil. The different realms are created around this magnificent tree. This chapter is dedicated to the Yggdrasil and the Nine Worlds of Asatru Cosmology.

The ancient Nordic people did not see the cosmos as only the Earth surrounded by the heavens above and the underworld or hell below. According to Asatru, the cosmos was a complex system of multiple realms and planes, including the human realm. All these planes of creation were interconnected with each other.

Before the start of time, Muspelheim, the fiery realm of fire, which was in the south, moved north to meet Niflheim, the icy realm. They met at Ginnungagap or the yawning void, and their powers combined. Muspelheim and Niflheim's union brought forth two beings, Ymir (whom we have spoken about in an earlier chapter) and Audhumla, a primeval cow of gigantic proportions.

The primeval cow licked the ice and created a new being named Buri, and from Buri came Borr. Marriages among these early beings, as well as sexless reproduction by Ymir, resulted in multiple generations of beings until three godly beings, namely Odin, Villi, and

Ve, killed Ymir and created the cosmos from his body parts. The cosmos created from Ymir's body parts consisted of the World Tree and the Nine Worlds. The World Tree, Yggdrasil, supported the Nine Worlds, who were separated by vast distances.

Rivers, valleys, hills, and mountains separated the Nine Worlds and were formed between them by the bark of the World Tree. According to Norse Paganism, the entire cosmos is much bigger than the Nine Worlds centered on the Yggdrasil. There are unknown worlds beyond the enclosure of the Nine Worlds. The Nine Worlds of the cosmos of Norse Paganism were:

- *Asgard* – The realm of the Aesir gods and goddesses.
- *Muspelheim* – The realm of the primal fire and the place where the Muspilli fire giants live.
- *Niflheim* – The realm of the primal snow or ice and the world of mists.
- *Jotunheim* – The realm of the giants and the jotnar.
- *Alfheim* – The realm of the Light Elves.
- *Hel or Helheim* – The realm of the dead.
- *Vanaheim* – The realm of the Vanir gods and goddesses.
- *Svartalfheim* – The realm of the dwarfs and black elves.
- *Midgard* – The realm of human beings.

Each of these nine realms has specific kinds of spiritual-psychological elements in operation. Let us look at the Yggdrasil and the Nine Worlds in a bit of detail.

The Yggdrasil

The Yggdrasil is the World Tree or the Tree of Life. This gigantic tree rises from the Well of Wyrd and forms the framework of the Nine-World cosmos accessible to the beings of Norse Pagans. The Nine Worlds reside in Yggdrasil's branches and roots. The World Tree serves as a conduit for travelers to move from one world to another.

Yggdrasil is frequently described as an ash tree, although it bears fruit and needles too. Most believers accept that Yggdrasil is a tree that cannot be compared with anything seen or known in the human world. Alternately, Yggdrasil could be a tree that combines the power and capabilities of all the mortal trees known to human beings.

Yggdrasil literally translates to "Steed of Yggr" or "Odin's Horse." "Yggr" is one of the many names of Odin and means "the terrible one." This name referred to the episode in Odin's life when he spent nine days and nine nights hanging on the World Tree to gain knowledge and wisdom until the Runes were finally revealed to him. Interestingly, an ancient Germanic custom of hanging sacrificial victims from trees could be rooted in Odin's self-sacrifice episode. Archeological evidence of the "Tollund Man" found in 1950 in a Jutland peat bog points to this kind of old Germanic custom.

The discovered body was so excellently preserved that it was possible to deduce that he was hanged ritually and then buried in the bog. This was the second such body to be discovered. About a hundred yards away, another body of a ritually hanged woman was also excavated.

A poem in the *Poetic Edda* called "Fjolsvinnsmal" refers to the Tree of Life as Mimir's Tree or Mimameid. It is also known as Lerad, a tree so huge that its twigs and leaves provide food for the goat, Heidrun, and the stag, Eikþyrnir, that live on the roof of Valhalla.

Three roots support the Yggdrasil. One of these roots passes through Asgard. The second one passes through Jotunheim, and the third one goes through Helheim. The sacred Well of Wyrd where the three Norns or Nornir (the three Fates) lived was beneath Asgard's roots. Even the gods had no control over the Well of Wyrd. The Well of Mimir (or Memory), Mimisbrunnr, lay beneath the root of Jotunheim while the well Hvergelmir (or the Roaring Cauldron) lay beneath the Helheim root.

The World Tree is an essential element to the story of Ragnarok. According to prophecies in Norse mythology, only two human beings would survive the Ragnarok, namely Lif and Lifthrasir. These two people would escape from the brunt of the war by sheltering themselves in Yggdrasil's branches and consuming the dew on the World Tree leaves.

Muspelheim

Muspelheim is the realm of fire and home to the fire giants; ruled over by Surtr or the Black one. It is located to the south of Ginnungagap. In Norse mythology, fire giants like Surtr are considered to be as close to pure evil as possible. Muspelheim, along with Niflheim (the realm of ice), joined together to create the first being: Ymir. It is believed that sparks from this realm created comets, stars, and planets. According to some sources of Norse mythology, Muspelheim fire giants are expected to fight against the gods in Ragnarok.

Niflheim

Niflheim or "Mistland" is the realm of cold and ice. Located to the north of Ginnungagap, Niflheim is inhabited by ice giants or Rimtursir. Niflheim is ruled over by Hel, daughter of Loki and a giantess. Odin appoints Hel to rule over Niflheim. Half of Hel's body is normal, while the other half resembles a rotting corpse.

Niflheim is divided into numerous sub-realms, out of which one of the realms is dedicated to gods and heroes. In this sub-realm, the goddess Hel presides over the festivities held for the gods and heroes. Another sub-layer of Niflheim is for the sick, elderly, and all those who cannot die in glory. The ones who die in glory go straight to Valhalla in Asgard.

The lowest sub-realm in Niflheim is similar to the hell in Christianity reserved for the wicked who will rot here for eternity. Niflheim is located beneath the third root of Yggdrasil and close to the river Hvergelmir or the "stream that bubbles and boils" and the sunless hall or Nastrand, which means "corpse strands."

In terms of philosophy and psychology, Niflheim is the plane of evolutionary impulse or telekinesis.

Asgard

The Aesir gods and goddesses' realm is Asgard, and it is fortified by strong walls built by a frost giant and guarded by Heimdall. The plain of Idavoll lies right at the center of Asgard, and this is the place where the deities meet for important discussions. Two important halls in Asgard are Vingolf, where the goddesses meet, and Gladsheim, where the gods meet. Valhalla, or the hall of the slain, is another hall of importance in Asgard. The warriors killed in battle are guided to Valhalla by the Valkyries, where they are prepared for the Ragnarok.

Asgard is at a higher plane than Midgard. Human beings can reach Asgard in multiple ways, including:

- The Bifrost or Asbru, a rainbow bridge that connects Midgard to Asgard.
- Gjallerbru or the resounding bridge in Helheim.
- Myrkvid or the mirk wood between Muspelheim and Asgard.
- The rivers flowing around Asgard. Thor uses these rivers, as the bridges cannot withstand his weight.

Asgard is believed to symbolize the highest levels of consciousness.

Vanaheim

Home to the Vanir gods and goddesses, Vanaheim is also close to Asgard and is one of the highest planes in the cosmology of Norse Paganism. Vanaheim is also referred to as the home of the Earth deities of fertility. The Vanir gods are believed to be more benevolent and compassionate than the Aesir gods, who are more passionate and love wars and battles.

The three prominent deities of Vanaheim are Njord, Freyr, and Freya. Vanaheim is full of beautiful mansions and palaces, similar to Asgard. Vanaheim is the birthplace of Njord, and he would return here after Ragnarok, one of the few gods and goddesses who was prophesized to survive the end of the world.

Jotunheim

Jotunheim is the realm of the giants and the jotnar. The giants create menacing problems for the people in Midgard and the gods in Asgard. A river called Irving separates Asgard and Jotunheim. The most important city in the realm of the giants is Utgard.

Utgard is the primary stronghold of the giants from where Loki ruled over the realm. Loki was a devious, dangerous, and powerful giant who appears in numerous stories as Thor's friend and companion. Utgard means "the world outside the enclosure" and is home to evil beings. Asgard and Midgard are seen as places shared by and accessible to both gods and humans, whereas Utgard is seen as the divider and is viewed as an ocean or river.

Other important places in Jotunheim are Thrymheim (the dwelling of Thiai) and Gastropnir (the dwelling of Menglad). It also houses the Jarnvid or the "ironwood." According to mythology, Jotunheim is in the north of Midgard. From a philosophical perspective, Jotunheim is the realm of might and force.

Alfheim

Alfheim is the home of the bright or light elves and is believed to be a place of splendid beauty. The elves residing in Alfheim are also considered to be very beautiful. Very close to Asgard, Alfheim is full of meadows, forests, and beautiful islands amidst large seas. It is considered to be a happy, sunny place.

The Elven race residing in Alfheim is similar to human beings, although they are taller, fairer, and live longer than humans. Alfheim was a gift given to Freyr when he was an infant and got his first tooth. Alfheim is the domain of the ego and the place of intuition and instinctive powers.

Midgard

Midgard is the realm of human beings and is believed to be located in the middle of the World Tree. Midgard translates to "the realm in the middle," which is the reason it is often referred to as the "Middle Earth."

Midgard is described as a middle world that exists between Helheim (hell or the underworld) and Asgard (the heavens or the upper world). Thus, Midgard forms part of a triad which includes:

- The upper realm, or the heavens.
- The middle realm, or the Earth.
- The lower realm, or the underworld.

Midgard was created from the flesh and blood of Ymir, the primal living being. Bifrost, the rainbow bridge guarded by Heimdall, connects Midgard to Asgard. A gigantic ocean where Jormungand the great snake resides surrounds Midgard. It is so huge and long that it encircles Midgard entirely and ends up biting its own tail.

Thor is the son of the Earth Goddess, and therefore, he took it upon himself to protect the people of Midgard. Being an Aesir god, he also became the self-appointed protector of Asgard. Thor was, therefore, the powerful protector of Midgard and Asgard against the marauding beings who sought to harm the two worlds closest to Thor's heart.

According to Norse mythology, Midgard was completely decimated in Ragnarok. Jormungand emerged from the vast seas surrounding Midgard to poison the land and waters with its venom. The sea lashed up against the land. In the final battle, almost all life on Midgard was destroyed, and the sea swallowed up the earth.

Midgard is associated with our conscious thought, the area of the mind that human being's access when we are awake. This realm also represents the path of spiritual and genetic evolution, individual growth, and the synergy of light and darkness as well as fire and ice.

Helheim

Helheim or Hel is the realm or abode of the dead. The Goddess Hel or Hella rules over it, and it's the lowest realm of the Nine Worlds. Resting far beneath the Yggdrasil, it is close to Niflheim. Not all parts of Helheim are bad and dark. Some parts are like an afterlife paradise filled with light and happiness and some parts of it are dark and gloomy.

Also, Hel is not a place of punishment. Primarily, it is a place where the souls of the dead rest. It is filled with the ghostly specters of souls that have died ingloriously or lived a wicked life. Helheim is also the home of souls who have broken promises in their lives.

Helheim is reached through three portals, including:
- The Hell Way or Highway to Hell or Helvergr.
- Gjoll, a river of blood.
- Gnipahellier or Overhanging cave.

The gateway to Hel is called Hel's Gate (Helgrind) or Corpse Gate (Nagrind), which is guarded by Modgud, a giantess along with her giant hound, Garmr. The gates of hell are toward the south, away from Asgard, whose gates are to the north. Gjoll, the river of blood surrounding Hel, is freezing cold and also has knives floating on it.

The only way one can cross the river is by walking across a bridge that is guarded by a giantess. According to Norse Paganism beliefs, if a living person walked on the bridge, it would create noise so loud that it seemed as if a thousand men were trying to walk on it, but a dead person could walk across the bridge without a sound.

In the northern part of Hel the mansion of the goddess Hel is located, which is called Evdinir or "misery." A wall called the "falling peril" or Fallanda Forad surrounds goddess Hel's palace. Below Hel's mansion is the place of punishment for the wicked called Kvalheim, and located here is a place made of adders or snakes. The wicked and evil people are sent here so that the poison of the snake drips on them.

Psychologically and philosophically speaking, Helheim refers to the collective unconscious aspects of the human mind. It also represents the human connection with nature and our ancestors.

Svartalfheim

Svartalfheim is the realm of the black elves (the light elves live in Alfheim). Black or dark elves are known as Dokkalfar in Norse mythology. Like the trolls, the dark elves are connected with "daveves" or "dvergar." Some sources state that this realm can be accessed through certain caves in Midgard.

As defined by Norse Paganism, the cosmos is based around Yggdrasil and comprises the Nine Worlds that spread across the branches and roots of this magical tree.

Chapter 8: Heathen Rituals, Shamans, and Songs

This chapter is dedicated to heathen rites and rituals and how they have undergone changes in modern times, even as new lessons, especially compassionate ideas, were learned and incorporated into the ancient culture. We start the chapter with the most important Asatru ritual—the blot.

The Blot

The blot is a Heathenry ritual where offerings are given to the gods. Exchanging gifts was an important aspect of early Germanic tribes and societies. Giving gifts was a way of making and maintaining friendships and relationships. Gift exchanges among family and kinsfolk were a way of bonding with each other and reflecting the responsibility of each member toward the community as a whole. Interestingly, the offering of gifts to gods and goddesses had the same connotation.

Norse Pagans believe that we are friends and kinsfolk of gods and goddesses. Heathens do not look upon their deities as masters, nor do they look upon themselves as being slaves to the gods. This approach means that the offering of gifts is not taken as a way of appeasing or pleasing the deities, but as a way of demonstrating kinship and friendship.

So, the next question is, what kind of gifts do the gods give to us? The Astruars believe that the most useful and important gifts we can get from our gods are courage, wisdom, spiritual insights and growth, a feeling of connection with nature and the cosmos, inspiration, and awe and gratitude for what we have access to in this world. Good luck is also an important gift that gods can give human beings.

Human beings give gifts of loyalty ("troth" is the archaic term used by Heathens), honor, and remembrance. The mutual exchange of gifts creates a rich and deep bond between gods and human beings and is beneficial to everyone concerned.

In addition to being a gift-giving ritual for the gods, a blot ceremony provides an opportunity for believers to get together and bond over their culture and tradition. The ritual typically happens outdoors and includes an offering of mead, which is kept in a bowl. For the uninitiated, mead is an alcoholic beverage made by fermenting honey with water and often flavored with fruits, hops, grains, and spices.

In a blot ceremony, the priests and/or priestesses invoke the gods and seek their help. They then use a branch or sprig of an evergreen tree to sprinkle mead on the idols of the deities. The offering is also sprinkled on the assembled participants. The ritual could be improvised as it progresses, or the priests and priestesses could follow a strict structure and script. There are no hard and fast rules for it.

When the sprinkling is done, and the gods invoked, the bowl of mead is emptied into the fire or the earth, signifying the final libation. Often, the blot ritual is followed by a communal meal, which forms part of the ritual itself.

Other simpler forms of blot rituals are also followed. For example, the concerned practitioner might simply keep aside some food for the gods and wights without the use of sacred words or incantations. Some practicing Asatruars and Heathens perform simple daily rituals in their homes, but for most people, blot ceremonies are performed only on special occasions.

Changes in the Ritual Over Time – In ancient times (during the Iron Age) as well as during the Middle Ages, the term "blot" referred to rituals involving animal sacrifices as a way of sending gratitude to the gods in return for favors received, but such kinds of sacrificial rites and rituals are inconvenient for modern practitioners and not aligned to their morals and principles.

Moreover, animal slaughter in most countries is highly regulated by the government under humaneness and compassionate guidelines, along with hygiene considerations. In fact, the Astruars of Iceland explicitly reject animal sacrifices of all kinds. There are many instances of sacrifices gone wrong, wherein the animals were not slain correctly and died in agony.

Therefore, nearly all modern practitioners accept the belief that such instances are signs of displeasure from the gods, which, in turn, could drive them to cause harm to the practitioners and their families as a way of punishment. And so, animal sacrifices are not part of the modern blot ritual.

The modern-day blot ritual is quite easy and uncomplicated and can be practiced by everyone. It is a two-part process, particularly:

- We give our gifts to the gods.
- The gods give their gifts to us.

In the first part, the worshippers fill the drinking horn with mead. This horn is passed around the circle of worshippers who have gathered for the ritual. Each member holds the horn with both hands. This stance reflects the transfer of the gifts of love, honor, and loyalty from the holder's spirit through the hands, then to the horn, and from there to the gods. As the drinking horn moves around the circle, each worshipper transfers his or her love, devotion, and loyalty to the drinking horn.

When the circle is complete, the drinking horn is given to the person who is officiating the blot ritual. He or she raises the horn (filled with the love and loyalty of the worshippers) and offers the gifts up to the gods and goddesses. The remaining mead is then poured out as a final libation to the gods. An important point to note is that the mead itself is not the gift. It is only a medium that holds the gifts of love, devotion, and loyalty of the worshippers to their gods.

The second part of the blot ritual involves receiving the gifts and blessings from the gods and goddesses in return. Again, the drinking horn is filled with mead. The officiating priest or priestess raises the horn high again so that the gods can infuse the mead with their powers and blessings, might, inspiration, spiritual guidance, and other gifts.

Now, these gifts and blessings from the gods and goddesses need to be shared among the worshippers. There are two ways that an officiating person can perform this ritual. In one method, the priest or priestess takes a big bowl, pours the blessed and empowered mead into it, takes a sprig or branch of an evergreen tree, dips it into the mead, and sprinkles it on all the participants and worshippers. The sprinkling symbolizes the transfer of the power of the gods to the people present in the ritual.

Another method is to pass the drinking horn filled with the consecrated mead from member to member so that he or she can drink the empowered liquid and get a share of the power of the gods and goddesses.

Blots can be offered to multiple gods and goddesses simultaneously, or to a specific god or deity for a specific wish or need to be fulfilled. While modern-day gifts from gods and goddesses are intangible elements like courage, honor, good luck, etc., in the olden days, blots were performed for victory in battle, a safe voyage, a good harvest, prosperity, and other tangible needs and desires of the worshippers.

In a modern context, our battles do not need axes and bows and arrows. But we still have our own daily battles to fight. It is perfectly natural to seek help from the divine beings to win such battles, and blots are a great way to commune with the gods and ask for their help in the form of wisdom and good luck.

A Simple Guide to a Blot Ritual

This section contains a detailed explanation of how to conduct a blot ritual in your own way to reconnect with your ancestors, gods, and deities and reach out to them for their help. A perfect setting for a blot ritual is amidst the beauty and splendor of nature. Here is a step-by-step guide to help you get started.

First, you must prepare for the ritual. Then, the actual ritual has nine components, including:

1. *Vigia* – The dedication.
2. *Helgia* – The consecration.
3. *Bidja* – The prayer.
4. *Blota (Also Called Offra)* – The offering.
5. *Senda* – The sending.
6. *Signa* – The blessing.
7. *Kjosa* – The choosing.
8. *Soa* – The consuming.
9. *Enda* – The closing.

Before we can go into these nine parts, it is essential that you get the setting or the location right for the ritual. The best and most ideal place for a blot would be a grove or amidst nature. It is vital that you feel a sacred and solemn connection to the location where you want to conduct the blot ritual. A few examples of such ideal locations are:

- A large tree that reflects the power and strength of nature.
- Near a running body of water that mimics the fountains of the heavens and the underworld.
- The top of a mountain, which signifies the site of Valhalla.

Certain trees have great significance in Norse Paganism. The oak tree is connected to Thor, the ash tree reflects the World Tree, and the yew tree is related to death and transformation. Another important element for a blot ritual is privacy. You must choose a place where strangers cannot walk in unannounced and suddenly interrupt the ritual.

Now, it is not always possible to find a place outdoors that suits all these requirements, especially in modern times; a temple or hof would be a great location. If there is no Asatru hof in your area or community, you can create a sacred place in your own home, centered around a "stalli," or a sacred altar, for the blot ritual.

Once you have settled on the location, then it is time to move on to the next step which is to gather the tools needed for the ritual, which include the following:

- Statues or idols of gods and goddesses you will be dedicating the ritual to and praying to. These idols are an excellent way to get your focus on the rite, and it gives you a sense of having your deities present with you during the ceremony. While it is not possible or practical to have the idols of the entire range of the pantheon of gods and goddesses, you can choose to have a couple that you feel connected with and use the same idols for the rituals.

- Mead is an important element of any blot right from ancient times. It was believed that honey mead was very sacred to the gods, as it had its origins in the fountains of the underworld. While there are commercially available meads, it would be special if you brewed your own at home.

- The three important tools for the mead include the drinking horn, blot bowl, and the "hlauteinn." The drinking horn made of cattle horn dates back to ancient Roman times. The blot bowl is needed to pour the mead later during the ritual. The "hlauteinn" is an evergreen sprig used to sprinkle the consecrated mead on the worshippers. Before you cut a sprig from the tree, it is vital that you ask permission from the tree by offering a libation of mead to the chosen tree.

Other tools used during the rite include:

- A sacrificial blade to cut the offering (in the days of animal sacrifice). This blade was used to scrape out the runes, too, as the incantations and prayers were recited.

- A ritual hammer invoking the power and might of Thor's Mjolnir, which was used to hallow items and elements throughout the ritual.

- A gandr, which is a staff or wand, which was charged and used for special purposes.

- The need-fire (a filament flame) contained in a portable lantern.

- The peord or a special box to hold rune tablets.

The runes can be inscribed using the sacrificial blade onto any sacred object or a piece of wood. For example, in ancient times, warriors would carve the runes on their weapons for victory in battle. Sailors would carve them on oars for a safe voyage. Midwives would tattoo or paint the runes on their hands, seeking help from the gods to guide them through deliveries safely.

The runes you choose should be directly related to your prayers and needs. It could be one or two rune letters related to the ritual, or it could be the spelling of a word in prayer. A commonly carved rune is the word "alu," which translates to spiritual ecstasy. Even each rune alphabet has its own significance. For example, the rune "Ass" or "Ansuz" relates to the gods' spiritual wisdom. If you are going to carve the runes on a piece of wood, then it would be good to choose the wood from the tree whose significance is connected to your prayer.

Once you have carved the runes on the object or piece of wood, use the sacrificial blade and scrape the runes into the mead, signifying the transfer of power from the runes into the mead. The next step of preparation is the use of the ritual hammer signifying Thor's Mjolnir, the most important tool of consecration in Norse Paganism. The hammersign ritual finds mention in the early texts dating back to ancient times.

If you don't have a ceremonial hammer, you can use your fist for this step. The hammersign ritual starts with placing the hammer or your fist on your forehead, saying loudly and boldly, "ODIN!" As you perform the hammersign at each place, feel the power of the Aesir gods flowing through your body and mind.

Now, move the hammer to your solar plexus area and say, "BALDER!" Then, take it to your left shoulder and say, "FREY." Move it to the right shoulder and say, "THOR." Finally, touch the object that needs to be consecrated and say, "Vingthorshammar Vigia" which translates to "The Hallowing Hammer of Thor, Consecrate!" This ritual makes our object holy and it is believed to be under Thor's protection and that of his powerful hammer.

The next step is to set up the altar or "stalli." The altar is the central focus of the blot and signifies Asgard, the home of the gods. A white linen cloth to cover your altar gives it a clean, aesthetically pleasing look. Lighting a couple of candles enhances the sacredness of the "stalli." You can arrange all the tools and elements on the altar in an orderly manner, assuring there is no clutter.

When your preparations are done, you can begin the 9-step blot ritual process as follows:

Vigia - The Dedication: A blot begins with a dedication of the altar and the ritual's sacred space to the gods or vigia. The officiating priest or priestess sends up prayers of dedication to the gods in the form of songs or hallowed verses, while the other participants use various responses at the end of each hallowed verse. Here is a simple example of a hallowed verse you can use in the dedication step:

> "We call upon all the deities and ancestors,
>
> To come and dwell in this hallowed space.
>
> To be with us while we honor you with our gifts,
>
> And give us the help and gifts we seek."

Helgia - The Consecration: In the consecration process, the sacred fire purifies the air of the sacred space where the ritual is taking place. The need-fire is carried around the perimeter of the ritual space as a hallowed verse is chanted by the participants and/or the officiating priest or priestess.

The need-fire is taken three times around the perimeter of the sacred space, and for each revolution, the hallowed verse is chanted three times. Hence, the hallowed verse is chanted nine times. Nine is the most sacred number in Asatru. An example of the consecration verse can be something like this:

> "We call upon the loving and noble gods and goddesses,
>
> To light up and sanctify this area of prayer,
>
> Keep it sacred and holy,
>
> And give us your blessings to complete what we have started."

Bidja - The Prayer: The bidja is the holy prayer of the blot ritual. It is usually performed with the rune Elgr or Elhaz. The participants stand erect and raise their arms over their heads in a "Y" formation as they focus on the idols of the deities on the altar. This segment is about connecting with the deities and gods of the ritual within the perimeter of the sanctified area. An example of a hallowed verse in prayer can be created based on your need at the time. Here is an example of a prayer of protection chanted during the blot ritual during Winter Nights:

> "O powerful and mighty Thor,
>
> Grant us protection and peace.
>
> Winter is upon us, give us courage and strength.
>
> Keep us safe and warm."

You can have hallowed verses to each god whose help is being sought in the ritual.

Blota (Also Called Offra) - The Offering: This step concerns the offering to the gods, which is the central part of the blot ritual. Different offerings are given to different gods depending on the needs and time of the year. While animal sacrifices were part of the ritual in ancient times, in modern days, mead is the most common and popular offering. Odin is believed to live and survive on honey mead only, and therefore, it is considered an ideal offering to the gods in any ritual.

Before offering the mead to the gods, you need to charge it with the hammersign. This consecrated mead is offered up in an offering bowl or the drinking horn with a hallowed verse, an example of which is below:

> "Gods and Goddesses of Asgard,
>
> Your friends from Midgard offer these gifts to you,
>
> In return for your protection and love,
>
> Accept this offering of gratitude and reverent devotion."

Senda - The Sending: Now, it is time to send the offerings to the gods. There are many ways to do so, and all of them use the four elements, including fire, water, earth, and air, to send the offerings. In ancient times (thanks to archeological evidence), we know that plates of offerings were submerged in water, buried under the earth, left hanging from a tree, or put into the sacrificial fire. Today, it is a common practice to pour the offering of mead on the earth so that it finds its way to the gods. An example of a hallowed verse for this procedure could be as follows:

> "We send these offerings to you,
>
> That will find their way to your homes in the heavens,
>
> Partake of our gifts,
>
> And watch and protect our world."

Signa - The Blessing: According to Norse gift exchange traditions, it is now time to receive our gifts from the gods in return for our gifts to them. The officiating priest or priestess dips the evergreen sprig into the mead in the offering bowl and sprinkles it on all of the assembled people. An example of a hallowed verse for this occasion is given below:

> "Hail to you, almighty gods and goddesses,
>
> We solemnly thank you for your blessings.
>
> All through the branches of Yggdrasil,
>
> May you always hear our call."

Kjosa - The Choosing: This step is about interpreting the message of the gods. In a blot ritual, the lot box or peord filled with runes is first offered to the gods seeking their message.

> "We offer these runes to you, mighty gods,
>
> We seek your message for us, powerful gods,
>
> Tell us what we need to know,
>
> And bless us with your wisdom."

Then, each of the participants picks up one rune from the lot box. The interpretations of the rune they pick are then used as guidance points in their coming days.

Soa - The Consuming: Sumbel is a drinking ritual that is often performed to consume the consecrated mead. The sumbel is described in detail in the next section of this chapter.

Enda - The Closing: This entire blot ritual is now in the concluding stage. The officiating person performs a closing ceremony allowing everyone to return to their mundane, routine world after their communion with the world of gods and goddesses, leaving the participants empowered and strengthened. This step involves hailing and thanking the gods for spending time with the participants and seeking their permission to close the blot ceremony.

> "Hail to the gods who heard us,
>
> Hail to the goddesses who heard us,
>
> We thank you from the bottom of our hearts,
>
> Watch over us and our world."

Sumbel

Sumbel is another common drinking ritual followed by practicing Heathens. Also spelled as symbel, this is a ritual drinking ceremony in which the practitioners raise a toast to their gods. Often, a sumbel follows a blot ritual and involves a drinking horn in which the consecrated and blessed mead is filled. The drinking horn is passed among the assembled practitioners three times, signifying the past, present, and future.

Odinshorn signifies our past, Thorshorn our present, and Freyshorn, our future. Some of the practitioners sip directly from the drinking horn or pour a little of the drink into their own glasses, and as each person does so, he or she makes a comment or a toast to the gods, according to his or her needs.

During the sumbel ceremony, toasts are made to the gods, goddesses, and deities. Verbal tributes are also made to the ancestors, gods, and heroes from Norse mythology. After this, oaths are taken with regard to future actions. Oaths and promises made during such ceremonies are considered binding for the oath-takers, thanks to the high level of sacredness rendered to the sumbel ceremony.

In a sumbel ceremony, the toasts made to the gods and the tributes paid to the ancestors help the worshippers connect with and harness their powers and use them in their own lives. In modern times, sumbel has a powerful social role to play in Heathenry. It is a place and time when bonds are cemented, political moves are made, peace is negotiated, and newfound relationships and partnerships are forged in the Heathen community.

Sumbel ceremonies are conducted with a focus on children, too, for which the drinking horn is filled with apple juice instead of mead. During the toast paying tributes to the gods, children tape pictures of apples onto a poster of a tree, which symbolizes the apple tree of Goddess Idunn.

At this point, it might make sense to summarize the differences between sumbel and blot in Asatru. A blot is a ceremonial prayer that can range from a simple individual ritual wherein only the practitioner lifts a mug of coffee or drink to share with the gods, to a large community event that happens on a football field. The small blot can be done individually at home regularly, while formalized Heathenism organizations handle the bigger ones.

Sumbel, on the other hand, is like a sacred drinking party where gods are toasted, and the participants sing their tributes even as the drinking horn is passed around. Each person takes oaths and boasts as the drinking horn is passed around. A group blot is an awe-inspiring experience, while a sumbel is a great bonding experience for practitioners.

Seidr and Galdr

Seidr is a religious practice in Heathenism that consists of a shamanic ritual trance. Scholars tend to believe that modern seidr practices could have been developed during the 1990s when Neo-Shamanism was developed and popularized, though older forms of seidr are described in many sagas. One of the most popular seidr practices of the ancient followers of Norse Paganism is referred to as oracular or high-seat seidr, which is described in Eiriks saga or the Saga of Erik the Red. This saga is an account of the exploration of North America by the Nordic people.

In the oracular seidr ritual, a seidr practitioner sits on a high seat. Chants and songs are used to invoke the gods and wights. Drumming, a popular element in Shamanism, is used to induce an altered state of consciousness in the practitioner. In this altered state of consciousness, the practitioner undertakes a meditative journey where they travel through the World Tree to Helheim.

The assembled participants ask questions to which they need answers. The practitioner finds these answers from Helheim by speaking to the ancestor spirits, and the divine beings that reside there pass the messages and answers on to the seekers. Some seidr practitioners use entheogenic substances to achieve an altered state of consciousness.

Glade is another Asatru practice that involves singing and chanting rune names and rune poems. Runic alphabets were used to write Germanic languages before the Christian influence. Chanting and reciting these poems rhythmically in a community helps participants get into altered states of consciousness, which, in turn, helps them to seek out deities and communicate with them. Although these poems were written in a Christian context, most practitioners believe that the themes reflected in them are of a pre-Christian era. Moreover, some poems are re-appropriated for modern Heathenism.

Festivals of Heathenism

In addition to the various blot rituals, different groups of Heathens celebrate different festivals based on their belief systems and cultures. The most common Heathen festivals celebrated by most groups include:

Winter Nights - Also known as vetrnaetr in the Old Norse language, Winter Nights refers to a three-day festival that marks the start of winter. Specific sacrifices and rituals are held during Winter Nights.

In the olden days, the King of Sweden performed a public sacrifice as part of a community event called disablot. Contrarily, alfablot was a ritual and/or sacrifice of the ancient times carried out in each household privately for specific local spirits and family deities.

Yule - Yule or Yuletide is connected to Odin, but the Christianization of this festival has resulted in Christmastide. Many customs and traditions practiced during Christmas today, including Yule goat, Yule log, and Yule singing, are borrowed from Norse Pagan cultures, or so it is believed. The above festivals find mention in Heimskringla and therefore, are believed to be of ancient origins.

Rituals and rites were an integral part of ancient Norse Paganism and adorn the modern version of Asatru. Sacred and hallowed verses, beautifully crafted ritual tools, food and drink, a deep sense of bonding and connection with other believers and the gods and goddesses, etc., drive present-day Asatruars to keep the tradition of rituals and ceremonies alive.

Chapter 9: Celebrate Like a Heathen – Holidays and Festivals

Celebrations and festivals are an integral part of Heathenism, and the Heathen calendar is replete with feast days, memorial days, and other special occasions. In fact, keeping and performing festivals is one of the primary duties of an Asatruar. Keeping these important days reflects the respect and love for their ancestors, gods, and goddesses.

Celebrating festivals and commemorating our ancestors and gods fills us with a deep sense of sacredness and takes us closer to the spirits of our ancestors and our deities. When we remember them on special days, they return the gift by providing us with protection, strength, and courage.

Most of our festival and feast days are aligned with the agricultural patterns of our culture and tradition, which, in turn, align our lives with the dynamism of climate and weather changes. Accordingly, every festival, feast, and ritual represents a transformation of the Earth as well as our souls.

Asatru has a compilation of all the feasts and festivals of all the Germanic and Nordic tribes that were considered important right throughout Northern Europe. In ancient times, some tribes kept certain feasts while others kept other festivals. The important thing about festivals in Asatru is not the time or even the ritual. It is more about the gods, goddesses, and ancestors who are hailed and worshipped as the Earth transforms around us. Let us look at some traditional festivals of Asatru in detail, although a couple of them were discussed briefly in the previous chapter.

Yule or Yuletide – The 12-Day Festival

The festival of Yule starts approximately on December 20th and goes on until the beginning of the next year. The word Yule is derived from "hjol," an Old Norse language term meaning "wheel." This is the period when the year's wheel is at its lowest point and is set to rise again.

"Hjol" or wheel is a direct reference to the Sun as a fiery wheel that rolls across the sky. It is important to note here that Yuletide celebrations predate Christmas and Christianity by thousands of years. Ancient Icelandic sagas are replete with references to Yuletide and also have descriptions of how this festival was celebrated. Yuletide was a time of joy, festivities, exchanging of gifts, dancing, and singing.

The holidays of Yuletide were considered to be the most sacred amongst all ancient Germanic tribes. According to Norse Paganism, this period marks the return of Balder from Helheim. It also marks the beginning of the end of freezing winters. The start of the Yuletide festival has no fixed date. But it is typically celebrated for twelve days and usually begins at sunset on the day of the Winter Solstice (the longest night and the shortest day of the year), which normally falls on December 20th in the Northern Hemisphere.

The first night of the Yuletide is called Mother's Night when Frigg and female ancestor spirits (collectively called Disir) are honored. The name also refers to the rebirth of the world from the darkness of winter. A nightlong traditional vigil is kept on Mother's Night to make certain that the Sun will rise again after the darkest night and to warmly welcome it.

The Norse deities are called Yule-Beings because, during this twelve-day period, they are closest to Midgard, the human realm. This is the season when even the dead return to Earth and participate in the festivities. Importantly, magical beings like trolls and elves roam freely, which can be dangerous for human beings. Therefore, the Asatruars believe in appeasing these beings with offerings of food and drink. The Yuletide period was a time of baking bread, cookies, cakes, and decorating every Heathen's home.

Disting

Disting (or Disablot) is a regular festival in Sweden (in this country, it was the first public fair or assembly of the year) and is also referred to as "Charming of the Plow." This ceremony takes place at the end of January or in the first or second week of February. In Denmark, the Disting festival is marked by the activity of furrowing the fields for the first time in the year. It is a feast signifying new beginnings. The ritual involves prayers to the gods seeking blessings before starting the work for the year.

Ostara – March 20th–21st

The Ostara signifies the Spring Equinox and is celebrated on March 21 every year. Marking the start of the summer months, it is named after the goddess Ostara, an important Germanic deity who embodied spring and the renewal and revival of life. The name Ostara signifies the east and glory.

The Ostara festival is a celebration of the revival of the Earth after months of freezing cold winters. Traditionally, homes are decorated with flowered, colored eggs, budding boughs, and branches, etc. The hare was the spirit animal or holy beast of the goddess Ostara. Slaying and eating rabbit meat was permitted only after taking permission from the goddess.

Holding and keeping the Ostara feast enhances the joy and happiness of the festival participants.

Some common folklore traditions that have carried on from ancient times and continue even today include:

- Fires kindled at the top of hills at the break of dawn.
- The performance of plays in villages and rural areas. In these plays, summer and winter are shown as people battling with each other, with summer winning over winter and driving him off of the stage.
- Effigies signifying winter as drowned, beaten, and burned to signify the end of winter.

Walpurgis Night or May Eve

Different countries celebrate it on different days, ranging from April 30th to May 1st. In Germany, Finland, and Sweden, May Eve is celebrated on April 30th. This festival is named after a lady called Valborg or Walpurgis or Valderburger or Wealdburg. She was born in 710 in Britain and was Saint Boniface's niece. She and her brother, Wunibald, traveled to Wurttemberg, Germany, where Wunibald founded the Convent of Heidenheim. His sister, Walpurgis, became a nun in this convent. She died in 779 and was anointed as a saint on May 1st of the same year.

Viking fertility festivals used to be celebrated on April 30th, and because Walpurgis was declared a saint at the same time, her name became connected with Viking fertility celebrations. Walpurgis was worshipped, similar to the way Vikings celebrated spring.

Walpurgis is one of the primary national holidays in Finland and Sweden, along with Midsummer and Yuletide. Large bonfires are lit, and the young people are tasked with collecting branches, wildflowers, and greens from the woods, which are then used to decorate the village homes. The young people are rewarded with eggs.

Heathens believe that Freya is the ruler of this festival because Walpurgis is the Germanic equivalent of Valentine's Day, and Freya is the goddess of love and witchcraft. In Scandinavia, the May Tree is taken out in a procession during this festival, a tradition that goes back to the fruitfulness procession of ancient Heathens. Fires are built in high places at night, and people jump over the flames for luck and good fortune.

Midsummer – Summer Solstice June 20th–21st

Midsummer is a Heathen religious celebration held at the Summer Solstice (the longest day and the shortest night of the year), which falls on either June 20th or 21st. Midsummer's Eve is believed to be the second most important Germanic festival after the Yuletide. On this day, the Northern Hemisphere is most tilted toward the sun.

Bonfires, singing, dancing, and speeches are some of the traditions of Midsummer's Night. Folk traditions like kindling a fire, making wreaths, burning corn dolls or human figures made of straw, and decorating the homes, fields, barns, and everything in greenery are followed enthusiastically. Midsummer is the best part of the year when planting crops is successfully completed, and the Viking ancestors have the time to undertake battle voyages. It is a time for risk and action, and to face and counter your fears bravely. Dancing around a large phallic maypole is an important fertility ritual associated with Midsummer.

While Midsummer is the high point of the year, it is also considered to be the time of the death of Balder, the god of a sunny and happy disposition, and the start of a period that slowly inches toward cold winters.

Freyfest or Lammas or Lithasblot – July 31st–August 1st

Lammas is believed to be an Anglicized word for "hlaf-mass" or "loaves festival," a Heathen occasion of thanksgiving for bread. Heathens celebrate this festival by baking bread in the shape and figure of Freyr, followed by its symbolic sacrifice and consumption. The first of August is the time when the first fruits of harvest arrive, and in Germanic traditions, the first sheaf is offered to the Heathen gods in thanksgiving.

In today's Heathenism, Lammas (otherwise known as Lithasblot or Freyfest) is dedicated to Freyr, the fertility god, and Sif (Thor's wife), whose long golden hair is believed to symbolize the yellow fields of ripe and ready-to-harvest crops. The warriors who went to battle after the planting season returned home at this time with their battle winnings. Freyfest is the day when the hard work of harvesting and preparing for the cold winters begins.

Fallfest or Mabon – Autumn Equinox

Fallfest is a festival of joy and celebration in the Asatru calendar and signifies the beginning of autumn. It is celebrated to mark the Autumn Equinox, which occurs between September 22nd and September 24th. This festival represents the second harvest. In the Germanic traditions, community bonfires were lit, and all the home hearths were extinguished. Each family would then light their home hearths again from the community bonfire. It was a time of thanksgiving for a good harvest.

Fallfest was the beginning of gathering and saving food for the upcoming winter months. It was the day that brought people and livestock together so that everyone could spend the cold, freezing winters as a community. To be alone in the cold winters was considered dangerous, since it would mean exposure to the harsh elements and perils of winter.

From the point of view of farmers, a bad harvest would mean a long and difficult winter with the imminent dangers of famine and a shortage of food. The fear of folks not surviving the season was at its peak during this time. In present times, however, the Fallfest has little or no significance.

Harvestfest or Winter Nights – October 31st

This day marks the end of the harvest season. On this day, people would butcher the animals that are not expected to survive the harsh winters, and their meat would be made into sausages or smoked for use in the cold months. Also referred to as Frey-Blessing, Dis-Blessing, and Elf-Blessing, this festival is the time for honoring land spirits, ancestral spirits, and the Vanir gods.

It marks the beginning of winter. It is a time when everyone was expected to turn his or her perspectives from outward to inward. According to Norse traditions, the festivities of Winter Nights were officiated by the woman of the house, and the last sheaf was left in the fields for the gods, spirits, and deities.

The Winter Nights feast was celebrated by telling old tales of bravery and accomplishments and focusing on future achievements. The Harvestfest celebrated the power, veneration, and importance of our dead ancestors. Moreover, it reminded people of the important tenet of Germanic belief that death was not scary or evil. For the Nordic people, death was not as important a topic to ponder over as much as living and dying in honor.

Other Festivals and Remembrance Days in Heathenism

There are many remembrance days to commemorate multiple martyrs and defenders of Heathenism. Some of these remembrance days are given below:

January 9th - The day to remember Raud the Strong, the chieftain of a Norwegian tribe. Raud the Strong was killed for refusing to convert his faith.

February 9th - The day to remember Eyvind Kinnrifi, who was also killed for not budging from his faith.

February 14th - This day is called "Feast of Vali" in modern Asatru, and although there is no connection between Vali and St. Valentine, many modern Heathens conduct rituals and seek blessings from this god on February 14th.

March 28th - Ragnar Lodbrok's Day, the famous event of Paris's sacking by the Vikings.

April 9th - The day to remember Haakon the Great, a great defender and proponent of Heathenism in Norway.

October 9th - Leif Eriksson Day, a day to remember Leif Eriksson, one of the first Heathen settlers in North America.

November 11th - This day is called the Feast of Einherjar, on which fallen warriors and heroes in Valhalla are remembered.

December 9th - The day to remember Egill Skallagrimsson, a highly revered Heathen warrior, rune magician, and poet of the Viking Age.

In addition to these festivals and remembrance days, multiple rites of passage are also celebrated in Heathenism, most of which are community-based and family-based occasions. The various rites of passage in the life of an Asatruar include birth (name-giving ceremony), puberty, marriage (swearing of oaths by the bride and the groom), and death (funeral rites).

Chapter 10: Practicing Asatru Today

So, now that you have a fairly strong background and understanding of Asatru, it is time to answer the question, "Where to begin with Asatru in today's world?" People in the initial stages of discovering their faith or those who have been following it for some time both have a lot of questions about what defines being an Asatru today, and how to move forward in the Asatru journey. This chapter is dedicated to giving you some answers to these questions.

The first thing you must do when you get a calling to follow Norse Paganism is to just listen and talk to your gods. Remember that in Heathenism, gods are your friends and kinsfolk, and having conversations with them can build your rapport as well as help you to understand what you need to do and how to move ahead.

Talking to your gods is a habit you must foster early on in your journey. Modern life is so rife with professional and social activities that we forget to have conversations with our gods. However, if you persist in building this habit, like other habits such as eating healthy, exercising, etc., it can and will become part of your life routine.

You can find gods all around you in the form of spirits. You can strike up a conversation with any of them whenever you want. There is nothing to be afraid of. You can simply go out there and start speaking to Odin, Thor, or any of the gods you believe in. A vital element when speaking to gods is to remember to do so with respect. Initially, you will not know how and what each god expects from you during a conversation. Respect is a safe place to begin your conversation.

For example, if you need to speak to Odin, the king of the pantheon of Norse deities, then it makes sense to see him as a leader or father figure who can give you the powers of wisdom and clarity of thought. When you summon him, do so with humility and respect and seek his guidance and wisdom.

With another god, for example, Loki, you could have a different approach. While respect is a given in every conversation, with gods like Loki, you can easily take an informal approach and treat him like a friend or ally. Loki is a god who will give you what you seek but will also want something in return. So, there is a sense of give-and-take camaraderie with this god.

Another critical element about having conversations with Norse gods is to have a purpose. What do you want to ask your god? Is there something bothering you? Do you seek enlightenment, clarity, or a problem to be sorted? Casual conversations like how your day at work went should be avoided because it would be wasting the time of the gods. Remember to value the time they give you when they come to talk with you. It is important to make your time with the gods meaningful.

The second step in your Asatru journey is to collect knowledge and wisdom. Do a lot of research and learn about the Asatru faith. What does it mean? What is its history? Who are gods and goddesses? Why are they the way they are? What sets them apart from human beings? What are the roles of the various gods in Asatru?

Learn about Asatru ancestors. As you learn more about the Viking and Germanic ancestors, you will find yourself unlearning many of the elements that got incorporated into the history of the Nordic people, wittingly or unwittingly. Remind yourself that the ancestors of the Germanic tribes were highly advanced and intelligent, built fast-moving boats, and were brave warriors. They traveled long distances and conquered many lands and imbibed the culture and traditions of the conquered lands. Our ancestors could have not done so much if they had simply been savages or fools.

The more you learn about Nordic ancestors and ancient tribes, the deeper your faith will become. A great way to enhance the depth of your knowledge in the domain of Norse Paganism is to try to rephrase the books, poems, and prose you are reading and studying. Also, you could check out if translating your lessons into another language will help you. Not only will this exercise build your skills in another language, it will help you get a deeper understanding of Norse wisdom, mythology, and ancient, forgotten knowledge.

The third step to becoming a practicing Heathen is to give offerings to the gods. The offerings you give in the form of mead, wine, meats, cheese, and other foods empower the gods, and in an empowered state, they are in a better position to help you when you need them. Again, it is time to reiterate the importance of gift exchanges in Norse Paganism.

When you give a gift or offering to the gods, they return your favor multiple times because they feel empowered by your gifts. Knowing what gifts to give to which god should be part of your research and learning process. For example, Odin is a god who only drinks and does not eat anything. So, if you offer him meat or cheese or something else to eat, he is not going to be happy, and the chances of him helping you in return are slim. Mead would be the ideal offering to Odin. You can get such important information only when you keep reading, learning, and researching the Asatru faith.

The trick is to start small. Begin offerings in little bowls, create your own hallowed verses, and seek the blessings of your gods. Don't forget to talk to them and ask them if they liked your offerings. The more you talk to them, the more you will realize that your gods are continually trying to send you messages and signs in different ways and through different people.

As you gain confidence in your ability to make offerings correctly, you can slowly and steadily enhance your offerings. There are people who started with a small bottle of mead and have ended up building firepits into which they throw steaks and meats as offerings to their gods through the fire element, but don't hesitate to take those baby steps. Start now, and sooner rather than later, you will find yourself expanding in your Asatru journey.

The fourth step in your journey is to connect with more Pagans and identify yourself with a community that you are comfortable with. Although Asatru is a sort of personal religion, it is also about ancestor worship, praying, dancing, and chanting together. It is about drinking consecrated mead together, and it is about worshipping and calling on the gods as a community. Therefore, it is important that you find your Heathen kindred and become part of it.

Also, the more you connect with other Pagans, the more you learn about your faith, and the deeper your beliefs get. Being part of a kindred is immensely useful in your research about your religion. Moreover, when other believers share their experiences with you, you will realize how similar these experiences are to your own.

It gives you a sense of identity and makes you realize and accept the presence of gods and deities all around you. You are able to counter arguments about being crazy to believe in the existence of gods. You know and accept their existence without question because you know others have had the same experiences as you.

The fifth step you should follow diligently in Norse Paganism is to have fun. Again, it makes sense to be reminded that gods and goddesses are your friends and family. You don't have to pray to them to forgive your sins and cry your heart out. You can explain your problems to them as you would to a good friend or a trusting elderly relative in your family and seek their guidance and wisdom to help you scale through the problems you face.

Our gods want us to be humans and have fun, including eating, drinking, and partying. They want us to embrace our imperfections and learn from our mistakes and keep improving ourselves so that we can lead increasingly meaningful and fulfilling lives. Our gods do not call us sinners who should be punished as a form of repentance. They teach us to learn from our errors and to incorporate the lessons into our future.

Finding Fellow-Asatruars

Here are some suggestions and recommendations you can use to find fellow-Astruars in your local community or the area you live in.

The Asatru Folk Assembly is a global organization with branches and representatives found in many parts of the world. You can visit their website https://www.runestone.org/ for more information. In addition to helping you in your research about Asatru and its customs and traditions, you can also go to their "Folkbuilder" page and connect with a team member. They, in turn, can help you find someone closer to where you live.

Another Asatru community with a presence on the Internet is The Troth https://thetroth.org/. You can register yourself there if you wish. Scout under the "Find your local troth representative," and you are likely to discover an individual or group closer to your place of residence.

Get in touch with the kindred in the cities closest to you and connect with them. Most of these people will have some idea of how to help you build your personal Heathen connection. Here are a few tips to help you get started:

- Do an Internet search with the words "Asatru/kindred/Heathen, [your city name]" using different search engines. You are likely to get some results from such searches, including names, contact numbers, and addresses. You can begin with this basic information.

- Use social media platforms to find Asatru connections. Many kindred groups have a dedicated page on most of the popular social media platforms.

- You can set up a local meet group using one of the paid apps that connect with other believers. Although you might have to spend money, it could be worth your efforts. Still, you need to use this only if the earlier attempts don't work.

- Another way of contacting Heathens is to get in touch with other Pagan believers in your area, such as Wiccans. Considering that many Heathens start their Asatru journey from Wiccan beliefs, these connections are likely to help you get in touch with practicing Asatruars.

The Kindred List

Here is a small list of kindred you can connect to, learn from, or contact to find your fellow-Heathens. You can send them an email and ask for their contact details or pose your questions:

Northern Mist Kindred - Located in Oakland County in Southern Michigan, the Northern Mist Kindred is a large group of Pagans with followers from different branches of Paganism. This group is focused on improving their knowledge and wisdom about Paganism and its varied belief systems.

Kenaz Kindred – This group follows and worships the pantheon of Nordic gods and goddesses and focuses on the conservation of our planet and nature. They accept people from all cultural and racial backgrounds into their fold because they believe everyone has the right to worship and follow Norse Paganism and its gods and deities. They believe in the Nine Noble Virtues of the Odinic Rite. They are located in Eugene, Oregon.

Shieldwall Kindred – Based out of Utah, this small Asatru group's primary aim is to expand their membership, gain knowledge and wisdom, and share it with people who don't know about Heathenism and its authentic nature. This group believes strongly in the Aesir and Vanir gods, and they respect the influence these gods have on Midgard and its people.

People from all races and communities are welcomed into this group, and they do not restrict entry only to people of Germanic origin. According to their belief, their gods and goddesses traveled all over the world, and therefore, everyone should be allowed into the Asatru fold. This group is dedicated to helping new Heathens build their knowledge about Heathenism so that they can imbibe Asatru values and principles into their lives and expand their mental, physical, and spiritual capabilities.

Northern Pines Heathen Kindred – Located in Northern Ontario, this Heathen kindred believes in self-preservation and self-sustenance. They honor and maintain a deep connection with their ancestors and the Asatru community. They believe in following the kindred honor code strictly along with the Nine Noble Virtues.

They follow and celebrate the traditional Asatru feasts and festivals, organizing rituals, ceremonies, and celebrations according to each festival. They believe in and follow the Asatru pantheon of gods, including Tyr, Odin, Freyr, Skadi, etc.

Hammerstone Kindred – This kindred group is a family-friendly group and organizes trips for members and their families to areas of interest. The members meet regularly to study and discuss Heathenry topics, including lore, mythological stories, related history, and more. The members hold numerous rituals and ceremonies to honor their gods and goddesses and share knowledge and wisdom with each other.

Oath Keepers Kindred – This group was established by a group of high school friends in 2015 in Wisconsin, and they have small chapters all over the state.

Northern Rune Kindred – This Universalist Heathen kindred allows entry to all people regardless of caste, creed, race, gender, and any other distinction. The gods and goddesses of Aesir and Vanir tribes are revered and worshipped. The members strive to live by the Nine Noble Virtues as they build their knowledge about Heathenism. They are based out of Herrin, Illinois.

Wyrd Ways Kindred – Based in South Jordan, Utah, this family-oriented kindred group welcomes all who seek permission to enter the fold and come with the noble intention of learning and expanding their knowledge.

Ulfr a Aesir Kindred – Based on a strict military discipline theme, this kindred believes that it is not for everyone. They practice a mixture of Asatru, combining some old ways with the new. The group is quite orthodox in its approach. Based in Missouri, this group allows entry to people of all races, creeds, genders, and communities, but you have to prove your worth over your birth.

Hrafn and Ulfr Kindred – This group has members who follow different Pagan beliefs. Some are novice Asatruars, while some others have been practicing Heathenism for many years. The members have found their way into this Heathenry kindred from Druidic paths, Witchcraft, and Native American belief systems. This kid-friendly kindred conducts blot ceremonies in open areas as often as possible. They are located in Topeka, Kansas.

Laeradr - This close-knit small community of Asatru is based out of a remote place in Norway. They are located on the island of Bjarkoy, an ancient territory of the Vikings. This island was a prominent region during the Viking Age and the Middle Ages. This kindred practices an inclusive, open-minded form of Heathenry and believes in human beings' deep connection with land spirits, gods, and ancestors.

There are many more such kindred groups, especially in North America. The list of Heathenry kindred is given in this book's Resources page, where you will find a more extensive list.

Worldwide Map of Asatru

The worldwide map of Heathens is a great way to connect with other Heathens too. Here is a step-by-step of how you use this map. The website link is given on the Resources page.

Open the map from the link and zoom in to your area. Even if you don't find anyone very close to your home, you will likely find Heathens within driving distance of your place of residence.

Moreover, even if you don't find anyone close to where you live, you can contact many believers (even if they live far away). They are likely to connect you with someone they know who, perhaps, lives closer to you.

Don't forget to add yourself to the map. Someone in the future might find you and seek out your guidance. This is your way of making the path of Heathenry smoother for new entrants.

If you want something badly, the universe will find a way to bring it to you. Therefore, keep your desire to become an Asatru burning through self-learning and self-development. The more you delve deeper into yourself, the more your knowledge about the external world expands. Continue your efforts to connect with fellow believers. Sooner rather than later, you are likely to meet with such people and have a great community to rely on.

Conclusion

It makes sense to finish this book with some interesting facts about Asatru, some of which have been discussed in detail in the earlier chapters.

Asatru translates to "faith," and believers extend the meaning to: "having faith in the gods." Asatru is based on an ancient religion practiced in Scandinavia as far back as the Iron Age.

It is a polytheistic religion with a pantheon of gods and goddesses who are worshipped. While there are formalities about how you pray to the gods, there are no prayers in the strict sense of the word. Each believer can seek what he or she wants from the gods in his or her own way. Gods and deities are imperfect in the world of Asatru, and they are seen as friends and advisors.

There is no prescribed scripture or dogma in Asatru. The Asatruars are continually building their knowledge and wisdom by reading *Poetic Edda*, *Prose Edda*, and other sources of stories. Also, archeological and historical evidence is used to understand Asatru better.

The structure of Asatru is highly democratic, with the members of nearly all Asatru societies electing their boards as well as their godi. The Nine Noble Virtues form the cornerstone of Asatru belief. These virtues include courage, truth, honor, fidelity, discipline, self-reliance, industriousness, and perseverance.

There are regular celebratory feasts and festivals and commemorative days right through the Asatru annual calendar, with the four blot rituals leading the pack.

Followers of Asatru believe in valuing nature, emphasizing the interconnectedness of everything and everyone in this cosmos. Asatruars respect nature and have dedicated nature spirits that are also given offerings and appeased if angered.

And finally, there are no proselytizing or forced conversions of any kind. Nearly all believers get an internal calling to learn about and follow Asatru.

Here's another book by Mari Silva that you might like

MARI SILVA
MYSTICISM
Unlocking the Path of the Mystic and Embracing Mystery and Intuition through Meditation

Your Free Gift (only available for a limited time)

Thanks for getting this book! If you want to learn more about various spirituality topics, then join Mari Silva's community and get a free guided meditation MP3 for awakening your third eye. This guided meditation mp3 is designed to open and strengthen ones third eye so you can experience a higher state of consciousness. Simply visit the link below the image to get started.

https://spiritualityspot.com/meditation

References

11 things to know about the present day practice of Ásatrú, the ancient religion of the Vikings. (n.d.). Icelandmag. https://icelandmag.is/article/11-things-know-about-present-day-practice-asatru-ancient-religion-vikings

A Guide to Norse Gods and Goddesses - Centre of Excellence. (2018, October 29). Centre of Excellence. https://www.centreofexcellence.com/norse-gods-goddesses/

Heart, H. at. (2015, July 15). *Spirits of the Land: Landvaettir, Wights, and Elves.* Heathen at Heart. https://www.patheos.com/blogs/heathenatheart/2015/07/spirits-of-the-land-landvaettir-wights-and-elves/

Kindred List. (n.d.). The-Asatru-Community. Retrieved from https://www.theasatrucommunity.org/

Metalgaia. (2014, January 20). *Three Asatru Perspectives: Universalism, Folkism and Tribalism.* Metal Gaia. https://metal-gaia.com/2014/01/20/three-asatru-perspectives-universalism-folkism-and-tribalism/

Nine Noble Virtues of Asatru. (2020). Odinsvolk.Ca. http://www.odinsvolk.ca/O.V.A.%20-%20NNV.htm

Norse Holidays and Festivals. (n.d.). The Pagan Journey. http://thepaganjourney.weebly.com/norse-holidays-and-festivals.html

Norse Mythology for Smart People - The Ultimate Online Guide to Norse Mythology and Religion. (2012). Norse Mythology for Smart People. https://norse-mythology.org/

Odin's Volk. (n.d.). Odinsvolk.Ca. Retrieved from http://odinsvolk.ca/

Temple of Our Heathen Gods. (n.d.). Heathengods.com. Retrieved from http://heathengods.com/find/index.htm

Vættir. (2018, December 22). The Norse Völva. https://theheart756621753.wordpress.com/vaettir/

Vikings, Paganism And The Gods. (n.d.). Medieval Chronicles. Retrieved from https://www.medievalchronicles.com/medieval-history/medieval-history-periods/vikings/vikings-paganism-and-the-gods

Ýdalir - Inspired by the North. (n.d.). Retrieved from http://ydalir.ca/

Printed in Great Britain
by Amazon